TO SLAKE A THIRST:
The Matt Talbot Way to Sobriety

Visit our web site at
www.albahouse.org
(for orders www.stpauls.us)

or call 1-800-343-2522 (ALBA)
and request current catalog

TO SLAKE A THIRST:
The Matt Talbot Way to Sobriety

PHILIP MAYNARD

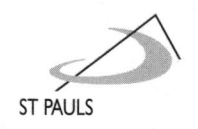

ST PAULS

Library of Congress Cataloging-in-Publication Data

Maynard, Philip.
 To slake a thirst : the Matt Talbot way to sobriety / Philip Maynard.
   p. cm.
   ISBN 0-8189-0843-2
   1. Alcoholics—Rehabilitation. 2. Alcoholism—Religious aspects— Christianity. 3. Talbot, Matt, 1856-1925. I. Title.

 HV5278.M29 2000
 248.8'629—dc21

                                                                00-025512

Produced and designed in the United States of America by the
Fathers and Brothers of the Society of St. Paul,
2187 Victory Boulevard, Staten Island, New York 10314-6603
as part of their communications apostolate.

ISBN-13: 978-0-8189-0843-9
ISBN-10: 0-8189-0843-2

© Copyright 2000 by the Society of St. Paul

Printing Information:

Current Printing - first digit   2   3   4   5   6   7   8   9   10

Year of Current Printing - first year shown

            2007 2008 2009 2010 2011 2012 2013 2014

In memory of my parents
Theodore Maynard
and
Sara Casey Maynard

Whom wilt thou find to love ignoble thee,
Save Me, save only Me?....
Ah, fondest, blindest, weakest,
I am He Whom thou seekest!

The Hound of Heaven
Francis Thompson

Visit these web sites:
WWW.MATTTALBOT.ORG
WWW.MATTTALBOTWAY.COM

Contents

Acknowledgments xi
Preface xiii
Introduction xix

Part One: The Matt Talbot Way to Sobriety

Chapter I: The Spiritual Dimension 3
Chapter II: A Higher Spirituality 9
Chapter III: A Matter of Power 15
Chapter IV: An Appeal to the Heart 21
Chapter V: An Uncommon Gift 31
Chapter VI: The Matt Talbot Way 35
Chapter VII: Getting Started 47
Chapter VIII: Markings Along the Way 57
Chapter IX: A New Life 65
Chapter X: Models for Imitation 73

Part Two: A Short Life of Matt Talbot

Chapter XI: The Early Years 81
Chapter XII: The New Matt 89
Chapter XIII: The Inner Man 101
Chapter XIV: Spiritual Motivation 111
Chapter XV: Matt's Heroes 117
Chapter XVI: Matt Talbot Today 131

Part Three: Other Uses of the Matt Talbot Way

Chapter XVII: Giving Up Cigarettes 141
Chapter XVIII: Controlling Your Weight 147

Selected Writings about Matt Talbot 155

Appendices

I: Summary of the Matt Talbot Way 157
II: Christ-Centered Prayers for Catholics 161
III: Non-Spiritual Practices 177

Notes 181

Acknowledgments

Even before I had taken my first drink, my mother told me about Matt Talbot and how his experience with alcohol could be drawn upon by anyone who wanted to overcome too great a liking for liquor. All of this I have written about in the Preface. The influence of my father on me was just as strong, though his role in my finding the experience of Matt Talbot as the key to mastering my own addiction was more indirect. Both of them played all-important roles of course in my religious and spiritual formation. By their love for me and my brothers and sisters, they had left an indelible impression on me; in matters where there is conflict of moral or life values, love for something—especially love for God—can be far more powerful than fear of something else. But it was the nature of my father's writings that had a singular effect in disposing me to being receptive to how the life of someone like Matt Talbot could help resolve difficulties that might arise in my own life. Without the unique and pervasive influence of my parents, I could never have written this book.

The role of my wife Agnes was entirely different but just as significant. It was her continuing love and patience and generosity of spirit, combined with a steady insistence that I had to do something about my drinking, that finally led me to the realization that the life of Matt Talbot held the answer. Over many years she had created and sustained the atmosphere in which the unique method of what I call The Matt Talbot Way to Sobriety could germinate and finally come to full flowering. Without her there would be no book.

The manuscript of *To Slake a Thirst* was reviewed by Anthony J. Tambasco, Ph.D., a theologian at Georgetown University. Several changes that he suggested have been incorporated into it.

Also, my brother Michael's wife, Mildred Maynard, a professional copy editor, read the manuscript, which now reflects her changes as well.

At the end of Chapter XVIII is a list of biographical works on Matt Talbot. Special mention should be made about three of them: Joseph Glynn's *Life of Matt Talbot* and Mary Purcell's *Matt Talbot and His Times* and *Remembering Matt Talbot*.

Within months of Matt Talbot's death in 1925 Sir Joseph Glynn wrote a pamphlet based on the recollections of a close friend of Matt's. Because of the intense interest this generated, he was prevailed upon to do an extended work, resulting in his *Life of Matt Talbot*, published in 1928. Mary Purcell's *Matt Talbot and His Times* first appeared in 1954. In 1990, she published a complete revision of the book, now titled, *Remembering Matt Talbot*. The writer gratefully acknowledges his dependence on these books for basic data about Matt Talbot.

Preface

It seems as though I have always known the Irishman Matt Talbot. As a young child, I first heard about him from my mother. She often received letters from her sister, who also lived in Ireland, which mentioned him. I was too young to understand precisely what the letters said about him, except that they seemed to increase my mother's admiration for him. Before coming to the United States, she had lived in Dublin for a few years but their paths never crossed.

Later, in my early teens, my mother spoke passionately to me about him, describing him as a poor workman who began to drink while still a boy, and after he had spent more than half of his life as a drunkard, he surprised his family and friends by suddenly giving it up. She held him up as the perfect model for anyone to imitate in overcoming addiction to alcohol. She suggested no special rules or steps to follow—one need only imitate the essential points of his life. None of this made much sense to me at the time. Anyway, why was she telling me this? I did not know what I wanted to do with my life, but whatever it might turn out to be, I was not going to let something as pointless as alcohol stand in the way.

My mother was concerned about the experience of her father. He had been a successful businessman, but towards the end of his life, excessive drinking caused him to leave his wife and the rest of the family. She was afraid there was something in my genes that would lead me down the same road.

About that time I was developing on my own a hostile attitude towards alcohol. Like many teenagers, I was interested in physical fitness. Everything I read in training manuals and magazines advised against the use of alcohol; gains on the track or in the gym would tend to be lost through its use. In reaction to these findings and my mother's warning, I decided to never drink.

After I was drafted into the Army, I went over a year without drinking anything alcoholic, even beer. But soon after my discharge I was prevailed upon by friends to have my first drink. I loved it and I was hooked, and I loved being hooked. I instantly knew that liquor had always been meant for me. A couple of drinks seemed to lift me above the world—I could better see and enjoy everything in it, better able to find myself and see where I might fit in. I had found a magic window to myself and to the world around me, and I was not about to brick it up. I knew I could never fully enjoy life without taking an inquisitive look through it from time to time, even though the insights were short-lived—invariably, fog, and then pitch blackness, would set in. As to my former convictions, why should I continue to pay attention to a silly resolution made as a boy who had never really begun to live? Surely I could not be expected to deny myself something so seemingly natural and good for me, even if the good always seemed to vanish so quickly.

For all its goodness, though, my drinking became increasingly troublesome. Whenever I could drink freely, usually only on holidays and at parties, invariably I would have too much. If I embarrassed myself I was able to neatly excise memory of it to the point of doubting whether the dreadful things really happened. The hangovers were awful but the delights of drink far outweighed the pain. To quit drinking never crossed my mind.

This is not to say that whenever I drank I always got drunk. I often enjoyed a few bottles of beer or ale while maintaining an essential sobriety. From time to time I would have one or two martinis at lunch with no apparent problem. But whenever there was plenty of hard liquor available, I usually wound up drunk, except when a business or social setting strongly suggested that I had to avoid making a complete fool of myself. But even on these occasions I often had too much.

My drinking sessions at home became more frequent and were getting worse, though I almost never went to bars. I drank to intensify the good feelings of life. I drank to snuff out the unpleasantries. And I drank out of sheer boredom. Whatever the occasion, I could always find a good reason. After work, I often arrived home only too ready to pour myself into a martini pitcher. My wife had been fairly patient through all this, but she was becoming increasingly exasperated. Finally, I agreed to see a psychiatrist, more as a way to pacify her than to quit. I saw five of them for extended periods over the years. They all gave the same advice—quit drinking—but I continued to drink.

Although I never worked and drank at the same time, the effect of drinking on my work was becoming more of a problem. Since graduating from college, I had almost always held two jobs at once, both in the same field. In time the second job became as important as the first, substantially increasing the overall load of my work. Naturally, I drank to relieve the stress, and as the demands of my work increased, I needed more time to drink but had less time to do it in.

Something had to give. I began to think the unthinkable. I came around to admitting that I was an alcoholic and had to quit drinking completely. Although I was not physically addicted—I had given it up countless times for weeks on end—psychologically, my fondness for it had a stranglehold on me. I couldn't imagine anyone liking the stuff more than I. Even though I admitted that I had to quit, I had convinced myself that I couldn't get along without it for long.

I tried Alcoholics Anonymous several times. Although I was

amazed, and often moved, by the stories members told of their past drinking and how A.A. was able to help them stop, I could never bring myself to accept the idea that I was powerless over alcohol, at least not in any permanent sense. I was willing to accept my powerlessness while I continued to drink, but I was determined that if I was going to give it up, my powerlessness would end with it. Otherwise, why quit? I might as well continue to drink and to take what enjoyment I could from it. A.A.'s motto of "One day at a time" may have worked wonders with others, but if I was going to quit, I would quit for good. I had had enough of fighting a daily battle—win or lose.

I also entered a medical program for alcoholics and drug addicts in which I attended weekly group meetings for six months, but it was no help. This is not meant as a criticism of either this approach or A.A., but simply to point out that they didn't work for me. Whether it was really I who was not willing to let them work is beside the point—for whatever reason, I did not, and probably never would have, quit drinking either way.

I was between the proverbial rock and a hard place: I had failed abysmally with A.A. but if I did not find a way to stop drinking soon, certain disaster lay ahead. This had a wonderful way of refreshing my memory. I had not completely forgotten what my mother told me about Matt Talbot—I had only pushed it to a far recess of my mind, ready to be recalled at some desperate moment. That time had finally arrived—I was willing to try anything.

But I had no idea how to go about quitting Matt Talbot's way. All I knew about him was that he was a reformed alcoholic and that his fame rested more on his life after he gave up drink than that he had quit. Indeed, his life become so exemplary that soon after he died, the Catholic Church began to consider him for sainthood.

When I began to check libraries for information on him, I expected to find something under a heading such as "The Matt

Talbot Way to Sobriety," but there was nothing. I did find passing references to him in a few books on alcoholism, but only in the context that he was an aberration that proved the rule, that the only sure way to quit drinking was by taking the same steps that I had already tried so unsuccessfully—go to A.A. meetings regularly. But I ignored these references—if my mother had been mistaken about Matt Talbot I was determined to find this out for myself.

After reading the only life of Matt Talbot that I could find, *Matt Talbot and His Times* by Mary Purcell, I began to understand why professionals in the field of alcoholism tend to dismiss him as a curiosity. There is little in his life after he quit drinking that the typical alcoholic can easily identify with. As a candidate for sainthood, he seemed to prove the rule that saints are best admired from afar. I realized that if I was going to be able to tap the source of his power over alcohol, I had to reduce his life to the essence of what it was that gave him such power, casting aside everything else as excess baggage. By concentrating on the essentials, and by making certain conjectures as to what motivated him, particularly when looking at his life as a whole, I was able to evolve a practical, step-by-step program that I call the Matt Talbot Way.

Before this, I had often wanted to quit, but I could never convince myself—nor allow anyone else to convince me—that I could do it. Not only had I deluded myself into thinking that I could never stop, but each failure gave me the perfect excuse to continue. And each failure reinforced my conviction that I could never quit. This time was different. I began to see the Matt Talbot Way as a sure way to stop—indeed, it became clear that I would never be able to stop any other way. Although I was frightened— and terribly saddened—by the prospect of life without liquor, all this vanished as soon as I took the first steps of the Way.

At first I could not believe that I had actually stopped—but I had and I was overjoyed. And it was so easy. The hard part, of course, was getting there. Since quitting, there has never been a tug of war: Should I drink? Should I not? When I was drinking, I faced these questions almost daily and the answer was almost always the same. But through the Matt Talbot Way I was able to convert this seemingly endless contest into one of no contest at all.

My liking for liquor is at a complete disadvantage in the new scheme of things. I still love it—nothing has changed here. I still look upon it as one of God's greatest gifts to mankind and to me in particular—that I had abused it is beside the point. But I can honestly say that I have never really missed it. The idea that I might some day begin drinking again has become unthinkable—at least as long as I continue to follow the steps of the Matt Talbot Way. Precisely what these steps are, and how any alcoholic can begin to take them, is what this book is about.

The Matt Talbot Way is not for all alcoholics, nor is it for all drug addicts. As Matt Talbot was a Christian he was able to find sobriety only in an inherently Christian fashion. For alcoholics and drug addicts to be able to follow his example, they obviously must be some type of Christian, no matter how lukewarm their faith might be at the outset. But Matt was not only a Christian, he was a Catholic. His way as I have presented it, however, is laid out in such an encompassing fashion as to be fitting for all Christians—Catholic, Protestant, and Orthodox. (This is particularly so for many Russian alcoholics, given the great faith of the Orthodox and their love for Jesus Christ.) Besides their Christian faith, candidates for the Matt Talbot Way need only a lively desire to stop drinking and a steadfast willingness to follow the simple steps of the Way.

Introduction

For all its remarkable success, Alcoholics Anonymous has only scratched the surface of the problem of alcoholism. At best, less than one of every fifteen alcoholics attend its meetings, and if you include "problem drinkers," less than one in twenty-five. This is no reflection on A.A. and its marvelous accomplishment. With its coming in the late 1930's began one of the most remarkable success stories of the century. Before A.A., doctors routinely wrote off alcoholics as hopeless drunkards. Now, successful treatment invariably requires continued participation in A.A. meetings. Alcoholics are given little hope for permanent recovery unless they regularly attend its meetings.

For some of those left untouched by A.A., though, the Way to sobriety inspired by the example of Matt Talbot may be the only approach that works. Matt was an Irishman who died in 1925. He was a hard-drinking worker who never let his drinking cause him to miss a day's work. He was proud of this, but he was an alcoholic nonetheless. He spent all his wages on drink, and when the money ran out, he did whatever was needed to get more, from begging to pawning his clothes, and, on occasion, to petty thievery. Eventually his steady decline into deeper dependency on drink brought things to a head—he finally had to admit that somehow he had to quit drinking.

Although Matt was weak in the practice of his Catholic faith, he knew that he ought to be able to draw on it in overcoming his liking for drink. But the usual Christian rationale that excessive drinking is sinful—better give it up now and avoid the consequences later—did not work for him. For a long time he had turned aside pious preachments from himself and others about where it was leading him. Not that he didn't fear God; it was just that fear of God or anything else could not override his fondness for drink.

Rather than try to overcome his addiction out of fear, Matt realized that he had to find a positive reason for staying sober. He had to elevate the contest between whether or not to drink to a plane where the temptation would be at a complete disadvantage. He couldn't satisfy his longing for alcohol simply by giving it up; he had to find something that outweighed his liking for liquor. Only a spiritual counter-attraction would do—only God himself, particularly in the person of Jesus Christ. Through his faith he developed a relationship with Christ that was to slake his thirst—he was able to quit drinking for good. Those who knew him were amazed that anyone so attached to the bottle could abruptly give it up. Today, much of Ireland takes pride in him.

That the Matt Talbot Way is inherently Christian should pose no essential problem for most alcoholics. The vast majority of people in the United States profess belief in some form of Christianity; much the same is true of alcoholics, though no doubt the percentage of believers is lower than for the population as a whole. Alcoholics who are also Christians—even though they may be weak in the belief and practice of their faith—are able to develop a motivation so powerful that they are able to overwhelm their old liking for liquor.

The Matt Talbot Way is not for all alcoholics, of course; but for many of them, it may be the only way they will ever stop drinking. It is for those who finally admit that they have got to quit but for whom other methods have not worked.

For alcoholics who are psychologically, not physically, addicted, the ability to stop drinking is not a matter of will power. If there is one thing these alcoholics can call their own it is their will. This becomes evident when observing them as they order their lives to make sure that they have the stuff whenever they want it, and if it's not there when they want it, to what lengths they will go to get it. What they lack is not will power but motivation—and the right motivation, at that—one that is stronger than their desire for alcohol. They have convinced themselves that there is no way they can get along without it. But once they begin to follow the Matt Talbot Way in earnest, they open themselves to an attraction which they discover is greater than their psychological addiction to alcohol. Then they become excited with the idea of finally being able to quit. The same obstinate will power that had always kept them drinking takes over and gives them the power to choose sobriety.

A.A. also uses a spiritual approach in its method of developing hope in a future without alcohol. It depends largely for its success on belief in God—or at least in a "Higher Power." But the Higher Power need not be God as commonly understood; it may be A.A. as an organization or the individual A.A. group or anything else the member chooses. Members are expected to admit that they are powerless over alcohol and then to rely on their Higher Power to keep them sober.

But some alcoholics, at least those who are Christians, see A.A. as not being spiritual or religious enough, in the sense that it does not directly draw upon their Christian faith. When A.A. was formed, all references to Christianity were carefully expunged; the idea was to make room for atheists, agnostics and others, regardless of their faith or lack of one. In recent years, however, Christian groups, both Catholic and Protestant, have formed within A.A. that expressly refer to Jesus Christ as their Higher Power. Although there are points of similarity between a Christianized A.A. and the Matt Talbot Way, there are also radical differences between the two.

And then there are those alcoholics who object to A.A. as being too spiritual, too religious. In recent years some of them have begun following Rational Recovery, a self-help program which maintains that an alcoholic can root out the irrational thoughts and beliefs that stand in the way of leading a sober life. Many of them are atheists or agnostics, but many more are Christians who prefer a secular approach. They attend meetings once or twice a week for about a year, using a talking therapy to overcome their dependency on alcohol.

Rational Recovery argues that since dependency is their basic problem, why substitute one dependency for another; A.A.'s Twelve Steps foster continued dependency, whether in the form of dependence on God, a Higher Power, A.A. itself, or the need to attend an unending series of meetings. It objects in particular to the first three steps, which require an alcoholic to admit that he is powerless over alcohol, to believe in a "Power" greater than himself that can restore his "sanity," and to make a "decision to turn our will and our lives over to the care of God as we understand Him."

Although there is a similarity between the Matt Talbot Way and Rational Recovery in that both insist the alcoholic is not powerless in overcoming addiction, the similarity ends there. Rational Recovery disdains the role of a "rescuing deity"; with the Matt Talbot Way, although God plays a role, the alcoholic is not rescued by him—at least not in R.R.'s sense. Rather, it is the alcoholic who takes charge—he is not powerless; it is he who works his own triumph over alcohol, but in a unique, Christ-centered fashion. To be sure, he is able to do this only by drawing upon the power that God offers to all Christians—a power that can be developed by actively growing in love for Jesus Christ. It is this power and how it can be developed that is at the heart of the Matt Talbot Way.

Prime candidates for the Way are those alcoholics who admit that they have got to stop drinking but cannot seem to find the motivation to take decisive action. Other candidates are those who have tried A.A. (or Rational Recovery and other approaches), and for whatever reason, either didn't like it or it didn't work for them.

Although the Matt Talbot Way is primarily for active alcoholics, it is not exclusively for them. Alcoholics recovering through A.A. may find that the Way's unique, Christ-centered motivation satisfies a need for which they had only a vague, uneasy awareness. A.A. and the Matt Talbot Way are, of course, not necessarily incompatible. A.A. members do not have to stop going to meetings but they may want to add the Matt Talbot Way to what they are already doing. In its own fashion, A.A. works extremely well for many alcoholics, even though many others are left untouched. The Matt Talbot Way simply operates on an entirely different plane.

Nor is the Matt Talbot Way just for alcoholics. It can work for full-blown drug addicts as well as those who only "experiment" with drugs. Whether they have abused themselves with alcohol or drugs or both, it introduces into their lives a powerful motivation that they will need if they are going to be able to stay off both for good. No suggestion is made that the Matt Talbot Way will be enough by itself. Drug addicts, more so than alcoholics, usually need medical treatment as well as extended follow-up help. Those in drug or alcohol treatment programs should not give them up in favor of the Matt Talbot Way. And after they have completed the formal treatment phase and are in Alcoholics Anonymous or Narcotics Anonymous, they should not stop going to meetings until they are absolutely certain that the Way by itself is enough, and even then it is advisable to taper off going to A.A. meetings.

The first ten chapters of *To Slake a Thirst* present a practical, systematic program to attain sobriety inspired by Matt Talbot's example. Because there are gaps in our knowledge of his precise spiritual motivation at the time he quit drinking, certain liberties have been taken in filling these in based on what is known of his later life. In a sense, his entire life after he quit drinking has been telescoped in order to capture his essential spirit and thereby distill the motivation that an alcoholic will need in following what is called here "The Matt Talbot Way to Sobriety."

For the follower of the Matt Talbot Way, the entire book, but especially "The Matt Talbot Way to Sobriety" section, is actually a do-it-yourself manual that should be followed step by step. And because it is a training manual, its key points are repeated many times to emphasize their importance.

The successful completion of the Way demands that the steps outlined in it be followed not just with dedication but enthusiasm. At the outset, however, the prospective follower may not believe that sobriety will necessarily be attainable. But if he is at least open-minded as he begins, and allows the Way to work its wonders with him, as he proceeds he will begin to see that the motivation on which the Way depends, which should be building within him as he follows the steps, can indeed turn any lukewarmness into the kind of fire that will make him want to give up alcohol for good. Besides their Christian faith, candidates for the Matt Talbot Way need only a lively desire to stop drinking and a steadfast willingness to follow the simple steps of the Way.

Although cigarette smokers and other persons addicted to nicotine don't like to think of themselves as drug addicts, they are addicts of a sort; their special needs in getting off of nicotine products is treated in a separate chapter. And people who have a problem with weight control, though certainly not addicts, have many of the same problems as alcoholics and addicts, though to a far lesser degree; for them the Way has been adapted to show how it can help them control their weight.

Part One
The Matt Talbot Way to Sobriety

Chapter I

The Spiritual Dimension

Getting a little high once in a while has always seemed to open up the spiritual side of man's being. Since Greco-Roman times and before, man has looked upon alcoholic beverages as a gift from the gods. The exhilarating effect of alcohol was thought to be caused by "spirits" from the other world. Dionysus, the god of wine, represented man's hope for a fuller and more abundant life. In the spirits released by the vine, he personified the power to foster a sense of mutual acceptance and solidarity among men, and ultimately, between man and the gods. But for some, opening a bottle has always been the opening of a Pandora's box: the spirits set loose also have the power to destroy.

Alcohol's allure comes from our innate human inclination to expand our spiritual consciousness and to see life in a positive light. Not only does drink stimulate the spiritual side of our nature, but it excites our sense of the possible. When sober, too often we may tell ourselves, "No. You can't do it—don't even think of trying." But a little liquor seems to expand our universe, and in the process, the "truth" seems clearer to us—the answer we may have been looking for: "Yes. Go ahead; you can do it. Don't worry about what the rest of the world says." But rather than just getting "answers" that may do little more than satisfy a false bravado, we may at the same time glimpse something of the mystery of life. Either way, we feel that we have found the truth, at least for the moment.

"Normal" persons take the delights of drink in stride. Though they may look forward to a drink with a certain eagerness, for the most part they can take it or leave it. But the alcoholic becomes so enamored with it, he does the only thing that seems logical to him: he tries to recapture—to bottle, if you will—the passing moment. Everything begins to revolve around drink. But the magic moment when he takes the first few drinks soon becomes little more than a ritualistic prelude to the poisoning of the spiritual side of his nature—to say nothing of the physical.

The elation expected from drink always seems to remain just out of reach. One or two drinks are never enough; if he stops then, the uneasiness which prompted him to begin only gets worse. He quickly learns that another drink immediately gets rid of his distress. And a few more will do whatever else is needed. Except during the early flush of his first few drinks, alcohol now only deadens his spiritual faculties. His capture of a bit of mystical awareness turns into a leaden, drunken obliviousness. Instead of finding a heightened sense of being, he becomes addicted to something that provides no lasting pleasure, joy or mystical insight.

For the first-time drinker, the delights of alcohol often seem to open up a whole new world, a world never before even imagined. Thomas Wolfe, in his autobiographical novel *Look Homeward, Angel*, has his young hero Eugene Gant exult when he gets drunk the first time: "It was, he knew, one of the great moments of his life.... Why, when it was possible to buy god in a bottle, and drink him off, and become a god oneself, were not men forever drunken?

He had a moment of great wonder… [as] might a man feel if he wakened after death and found himself in Heaven."[1]

Eugene's exuberance is typical of the alcoholic-to-be upon taking his first drink, though he may have a while to go before full-scale alcoholism sets in. A Catholic priest describes how the Eugene Gants of the world eventually find only frustration and despair as they return again and again to explore their newfound Heaven: "The alcoholic is not running away from life, he is seeking it, seeking it more abundantly.… On his first sizable drink… he experiences a high surge of feeling, a strong exaltation. 'This is it.' This is the life which you have been seeking. This is Truth and Good. This is a glimpse of eternity. It almost says to him, 'This is a little bit of God.'… At last there may come the realization that he cannot find his happiness in alcohol. In remorse he screams, 'This is *not* it. This is *not* Truth, *not* Good, *not* the more abundant life for which I am looking.' But he is powerless to do anything about it."[2]

Drink deludes the alcoholic into thinking he has found more than just a keener sensitivity to things of the spirit; he is fooled into believing he has hit upon the key to an easy transcendence over the world. But what he may want is not so much a heightened spirituality as a sense of power, a need to reduce the world and all that is in it to his domination. What he ultimately finds at the bottom of the bottle is neither spirituality nor power—rather, a deadening of the spirit and powerlessness over alcohol and himself. Nevertheless, if he is ever to overcome his addiction, he will almost certainly have to enlist spiritual forces in the battle. He must learn how to tap the same spiritual side of his nature that may have contributed to his becoming overly fond of alcohol in the first place.

Carl Jung saw the spiritual connection. In the early 1930's, he treated Roland, a long-term alcoholic who was a friend of Bill Wilson, soon to co-found Alcoholics Anonymous. Years later, Jung related in a letter to Wilson how he had told Roland that his situation was hopeless unless there were profound changes brought about by a genuine spiritual or religious conversion. Jung explained that Roland's "craving for alcohol was the equivalent on a low level of the spiritual thirst of our being for wholeness, expressed in medieval language: the union with God. ('As the hart panteth after the water brooks, so panteth my soul after thee, O God.' Psalm 42:1)."[3]

Roland found the religious and spiritual conversion that Jung had recommended, and with conversion came sobriety. He is often referred to as one of the pre-founders of Alcoholics Anonymous because of the influence he had on Bill Wilson. Years later, Wilson wrote to Jung that a spiritual conversion had been instrumental in his own recovery, and how, as a result, he came to found A.A.

Belief in God "as we understand Him" is basic to A.A.'s program. But such a God need be nothing more than what members call their "Higher Power"—some source of power of their own choosing outside of themselves. From the very first, A.A. fiercely guarded its nondenominationalism even though most of its first members were Christians. It wanted to be open to all alcoholics, even atheists and agnostics, as well as Jews and other non-Christians. In recent years, however, there have been a few groups of Christians, both Protestant and Catholic, which have expressly Christianized the program by recognizing Jesus Christ as their "Higher Power." The central office of A.A. has acquiesced to this. Other A.A. groups, however, have removed anything that could be construed as religious.

Once the alcoholic begins to rely upon God or his Higher Power, he will at last have found the means to keep from drinking. And if the traditional idea of God is not acceptable to him, then the laws of nature, science, or A.A. itself can be his Higher Power—anything that symbolizes resources of power outside of himself that he can rely on. But first he must admit he is powerless over alcohol; only then can he begin to make a completely fresh start by turning to his Higher Power.

Whether a member stays sober does not depend on raw will power; rather, it comes about because he constantly keeps before himself the underlying reasons why he wants to stop drinking and to stop permanently. By going to meetings, these reasons are burned into his conscious and subconscious mind. He hears other members tell and retell their stories of how drink brought them low and how A.A. gave them hope for a new life. If he wishes, he may tell his own story. All this reminds him of what will happen if he starts drinking again—he sees himself losing his health, job, family and home. Most important, meetings give him the chance to see and listen to fellow members. Rubbing shoulders with reformed alcoholics inspires him to really believe that he too will be able to live a full and rewarding life free of alcohol. It is this that keeps him in A.A. and away from alcohol.

A new member is urged to get a flying start by attending "ninety meetings in ninety days." After this, he is strongly advised to continue attending regular meetings in order to reinforce his newfound determination to stay sober. A member attends an average of more than two meetings a week according to A.A.'s own statistics, though some members find that they must go daily. After about five years he may go to fewer and fewer meetings. He may even be tempted to stop going altogether; but everyone connected with A.A. warns that if he does this, it is only a matter of time before he picks up his drinking where he left off. Most old-timers see a lifelong need to attend one or two meetings every week.

Although he may have been in A.A. for years, he never lets himself forget the sense of powerlessness that brought him to A.A. in the first place. He stays sober "One day at a time." Today is the only day he can do anything about, and today he decides he will not drink. Whether he will drink tomorrow is something to worry about tomorrow. Once he admits that he is powerless over alcohol, he is ready to become completely dependent upon a source of power outside of himself: God or his Higher Power—often A.A. itself.

Without question, the grace of God plays an indispensable role in the million success stories of A.A. Each story comes down to an alcoholic's determination to stay away from drink—though it may be only one day at a time. He may have to refresh that determination by regularly attending A.A. meetings. Still, drawing on the grace of God, it is *his* gutsy decision to keep going to meetings and to not drink. And each personal triumph becomes an inspiration to other alcoholics that they can do it too.

For most alcoholics, however, A.A. simply does not work. According to surveys (including those conducted periodically by A.A. itself), about half of those who begin to attend A.A. meetings for the first time remain less than three months, and about seventy-five percent eventually drop out and continue with their drinking. This is no reflection on A.A. and its marvelous accomplishment as it cannot be expected to work for all alcoholics, considering their diversity and the sheer obstinacy of most of them. Rather, what is astonishing is the vast number of lives it has reclaimed—especially when you consider that before A.A., alcoholics were usually given up as hopeless.

Chapter II

A Higher Spirituality

I<small>F YOU ARE AN ALCOHOLIC WHO HAS TRIED</small> A.A. <small>WITHOUT SUCCESS</small>, the Matt Talbot Way may be the approach that will work for you. It may be the only way you will ever develop a motivation powerful enough to make you want to quit. Once you get to know what it's about and decide to follow it in earnest, you can proceed with a quiet confidence knowing that it is only a matter of time before your drinking becomes a thing of the past. For some, this comes about almost immediately; for others, days or weeks, and longer, of preparation may be needed. In any event, to succeed you must dedicate yourself to developing the same kind of motivation that Matt Talbot had, though not necessarily to the same degree.

Matt began to drink before he was in his teens and was soon a confirmed drunkard. Although drinking was the most important thing in his life, it was never a solitary matter. He was almost as fond of his drinking buddies as he was of drink itself. What he enjoyed most in life was drinking with them in one of the pubs in Dublin. Every payday he turned over his entire wages to the pub owner with instructions to dole out drinks to him as long as the money lasted. By midweek the money would be gone, and he would wheedle drinks from his companions and strangers any way he could. He never brought any money home—home was only a place to spend a few hours before he went back to work to earn more drinking money.

Matt kept this up until he was twenty-eight years old. Then came one Saturday, ordinarily a payday. He had not worked for a week but had spent his time drinking heavily; now he was broke and thirsty as ever. He had no pay coming, of course, but he quite naturally thought he could count on his buddies to buy him a few drinks when they got paid. But they turned him down cold. His pride was crushed, but at least it made him reflect on their shallowness and his misplaced affection for liquor—he resolved that somehow he had to give up both.

Although Matt was a Catholic, with his early drinking he had become careless in the practice of what little faith he had. Still, he had enough of it to draw upon to quit drinking. Although his drinking companions had proved themselves false, he was still the same sociable sort of person who needed friends. So he went about making a new Friend. He knew that he couldn't satisfy his longing for alcohol simply by giving it up. He was able to slake his thirst only by developing another taste. Through prayer he cultivated a friendship and love for Jesus Christ. He took to heart his words: "If any one thirst, let him come to me and drink" (John 7:37). From now on he would drink from his cup, leaving no room for alcohol. His natural fondness for alcohol was simply overwhelmed.

To bring about this radical reordering of his life, Matt began to follow a methodical spiritual program. He started slowly but over the years, added more and more. Eventually, he was saying a formidable array of daily prayers. Most of the prayers were selected because they were an effective way to meditate on the events of the life of Jesus, especially his Passion. In this way he grew in love for him and was transformed by that love.

Matt never wore his life of prayer on his sleeve. His acquaintances saw him simply as a good man who led a quiet uneventful life, though unusually dedicated to the practice of his faith. He died in 1925 at the age of sixty-nine. Because of the suddenness of his death, the extent of his spiritual life was revealed in a dramatic fashion—more about that later. Within a year, all Ireland was marveling at him. Six years later, the Catholic Church began the slow process of determining whether to canonize him as a saint.

As part of that process, in 1975 the Church declared that he had practiced all the Christian virtues to a "heroic" degree and gave him the title "Venerable." This means that he is a hero or model fit to be imitated by all, especially alcoholics. Whether or not he will be raised to full sainthood, he has already become a symbol to many of the power of the spirit when dealing with alcoholism. But if he is to be something more than a mere symbol, he cannot be perceived as just a quaint saint-to-be; he must be seen as a flesh-and-blood person upon whom alcoholics can model themselves in a practical way.

Before he can be imitated in a practical way, the elements of his life must be rigorously sifted and those that are superfluous to the needs of the alcoholic set aside. What remains is the essential Matt Talbot. It is on this essence—the sober Matt Talbot and his life of prayer—that the Matt Talbot Way is based.

Matt Talbot's underlying motivation in giving up drink was love of God. At the time he quit drinking, however, this love had not reached its full flowering. But with prayer and meditation—which steadily increased over his lifetime—he became consumed with this love, particularly for the person of Jesus Christ. Indeed, the simplest way to sum up Matt—as with other saints—is to say that he had an all-consuming love of God.

Since his approach is essentially a Christian one, Matt's motivation in following a life of sobriety is something that can be copied not only by Catholics but by all Christians. No matter how weak their faith may be at the outset—assuming that the seed of faith is real, only that it has not yet come to full flowering—they can follow his Way with confidence that they will succeed once they really commit themselves to it. Probably no one will reach the level of Matt Talbot; nevertheless, those who steadfastly follow his example will eventually reach a point where they too will be able to give up drink for love of God. It is the essence of Matt's motivation that they must develop, not necessarily its degree.

Prayer helped Matt to see where he wanted to go, and it was his means to get there. God always hears our prayers, but in his own good time and fashion—often in a way completely different from what we had in mind. Matt cast his prayers—particularly during his later life—so that God had to answer them precisely as he had framed them. He prayed for what God most wanted him to have—that which was his for the asking.

Matt's prayers were irresistible to God because he made God the object of his prayers. This follows naturally with prayers of love, adoration, praise and thanksgiving. But even with prayers of petition, when Matt wanted something of a spiritual nature, he still made him the object of his prayers. Except in moments of crisis or when petitioning him for the needs of others, his method of praying (at least after his initial phase of learning to live without drink) was to express his love for him—particularly for the person of Jesus Christ—and to ask that this love might grow, rather than to pray for mere righteousness of conduct, such as sobriety or the virtue of temperance.

But prayer alone was not enough for Matt. He believed that if the Incarnation was true, and Christ had really suffered and died for all mankind, including himself, he should set no limit on his love for him or on how he should express it. A favorite prayer of his was that he might "obtain a share of his [Christ's] folly"—that like St. Paul he might become a fool for Christ's sake. Matt realized that he had within him the power to express his growing love for Christ in a very special way: he would do without drink as an act of love for him.

There is no doubt that drink can be a fitting gift to God, even though it had brought Matt low. All of God's creation is good, even if man constantly tries to corrupt it. The fact that Matt had abused drink was beside the point—its essential goodness remained unsullied. It would seem that his little folly was the gift to God of what gave him the greatest pleasure. Because of his love and admiration for the crucified Christ offering himself to his Father for him and for the rest of mankind, Matt made his own gift to him of the delights of drink.

One way to understand Matt's giving up drink is to think of him as approaching God with the innocent guile of a child who is secretly preparing a gift for his father, a child who even goes to the father asking for the money or materials needed to provide the gift, while keeping the purpose secret—though the father usually knows what the child is up to. Matt went about "secretly" preparing his special gift for his Father. To be able to make such a gift, it had to spring from his increasing love for Christ—it was this that gave him the power to quit. Worldly, ulterior motives would not do, though he might use these as a prod to move himself to the point of quitting. Indeed, he used the rejection by his drinking buddies as the proximate cause that resulted in his taking a "pledge" to quit drinking for three months.

Though his pledge was the first step in beginning a life of sobriety, when we look at his life as a whole, it was love of God that kept him sober. He completely changed the underlying motivation of his life. Before, everything revolved around drink—he worked for it, enjoyed it, and then slept and rested for the next day of more work and drink—all repeated seemingly without end. Now he would do everything for love of God.

In time, Matt's desire for drink faded into the background. But he never forgot how fond he was of alcohol, nor did he want to forget. The delights of drink that he was forgoing were to be a conscious, continuing daily gift throughout his lifetime. The remembered pleasures only made his gift more deeply felt. The only thing he asked of God was that he continue to grow in love for him. Only with that love did he have the power to slake his thirst—to continue making a gift to him of what he constantly prepared "in secret." He would do without drink for love of Jesus. This was the best way for him to express his love and compassion for the crucified Christ, of whom the Psalmist wrote:

"Insults have broken my heart, so that I am in despair. I looked for pity, but there was none; and for comforters, but I found none. They gave me poison for food, and for my thirst they gave me vinegar to drink" (Psalm 69:20-21).

Matt answered the call for a comforter. He knew that Christ's agony in the garden of Gethsemane was due, in part at least, to man's sins that were yet in the future. Couldn't these sins have been foreseen by Christ as the Son of God? Couldn't he have foreseen future expressions of love for him, which would have been a comfort and an encouragement to him in his agony?[1] Matt spent the rest of his life going back in time, bringing with him a special balm: a gift of love for the suffering Christ.

Chapter III

A Matter of Power

ENOUGH IS NEVER ENOUGH. HERE LIES HOPE FOR MANY ALCOHOLICS. The sheer excess of their drinking may eventually precipitate a crisis. At last they may be compelled to admit that they can't control it and have got to quit somehow. Regardless of what might bring you to this point, whether it is forced on you by family or employer, or simply because of some internal wisdom or spiritual light, you take that all-important first step. You admit to yourself—and possibly to others—that your drinking is out of hand and you have got to do something about it.

Still, if you are to be able to put alcohol behind you for good, you will almost certainly need help. For some, joining A.A. will be enough; others may need to go through a rehabilitation program that includes continuing participation in A.A.

Although these first steps are critical, what comes next in some ways is even more so. To quit drinking and then to take it up later with renewed vigor—and to repeat this again and again—in some ways is worse than never stopping at all. Failure becomes ingrained as you gradually accept the idea that drink has a permanent hold on you.

Regardless of what makes you face up to your situation during those first days of doing without drink, you must become deeply and powerfully motivated if you are going to be able to quit for good. If you are a Christian, however, you have within your grasp (though you probably don't realize it) a means of developing a motivation so powerful that it will overwhelm your desire to drink. Matt Talbot has shown that it can be done.

But don't confuse the Matt Talbot Way with the movement in recent years of some groups that have Christianized their participation in A.A. In place of God or their "Higher Power," these A.A. groups substitute Jesus Christ. It is Jesus who will keep them sober—provided they regularly attend meetings and follow A.A.'s Twelve Steps. Although both approaches to alcoholism are innately Christian, there are key differences. These come down largely to questions of self-identity and power. If you admit that you are an alcoholic and are powerless over alcohol—and you probably are as you contemplate following the Matt Talbot Way —must you forever see yourself as what you may have been? If you are able to quit drinking, will you continue to be powerless over alcohol?

With A.A., a member adopts what is fundamentally a passive role as he relies on some power or force outside of himself to keep him sober. Just go to meetings, follow the Twelve Steps, and he can rely on this outside power—God, Jesus Christ, a Higher Power, A.A. itself—to do what he seems unable to do for himself. Even though the A.A. member is able to follow a new life without drink, his sense of power in relation to alcohol is strictly limited. He is cautioned to avoid committing himself to long-term sobriety—just stay sober "One day at a time."

He identifies himself with his past—"I am Joe Doakes, an alcoholic." No matter how long Joe may be in A.A., even if for half a lifetime and sober all the while, he continues to see himself in relation to what he did and what he was before he joined—"Once an alcoholic, always an alcoholic." Although continued identification with this former self works well for most members of A.A., it has no place in the Matt Talbot Way.

With the Matt Talbot Way, it's not just a matter of how you view your past self; rather, what sort of person have you become? Because of the love for Christ that develops in you, and the commitment that that love prods you to make, alcohol no longer has any power over you. You are finally able to take control of your life. You don't wait passively for some outside force or power to stop you from drinking. Although the power to do anything comes from God, and he gives you the power to choose to love him or not, it is you who must choose to do so—and not just in an abstract way that might not have any real substance. Talk is cheap, but you prove your love by action.

By accepting God's offer to love him—not just by *passively* believing in Jesus Christ, but by *actively* developing your love for him, and then expressing that love by choosing to do without liquor—you are transformed through Christ. This comes about because of the power unleashed within you that flows directly from your love of Christ and the way you express that love. You have become a partner in the creation of this new self — a co-creator with the Creator, if you will.

Rather than passively praying to God to stop you from drinking, you actively reach out and take what God has been offering you all along. What you take is not sobriety, but rather love of Christ. Then it is up to you, by an express act of your inmost self, to use the power flowing from that love to quit drinking.

Rational Recovery also disdains the powerlessness that A.A. insists is an alcoholic's perpetual lot. It maintains that by using his rational faculties, an alcoholic can learn to overpower alcohol, rather than be overpowered by it. Notwithstanding the Christ-centered nature of the Matt Talbot Way, its approach is also essentially *rational*. Once the Incarnation and all that it entails is accepted as true—a matter of faith, of course—the follower of the Matt Talbot Way *reasons* that there should be no limit to his love for Christ. What could be more logical than to express that love by giving up the pleasures of drink solely as an act of love for him?

What makes any alcoholic actually quit? It comes down to a question of motivation. With both A.A. and Rational Recovery, the motivation is of the *natural* order: if the alcoholic doesn't stop drinking, he won't be able to enjoy the good life; he could well lose his health, family, home and job. Because he doesn't want to lose these good things, he decides to stop drinking by joining A.A. or Rational Recovery. The trouble is that even though he has made a certain commitment to sobriety, he is up against a powerful motivation on the other side: Why not continue doing what he has always enjoyed in the past? Just keep on drinking for all the old reasons and tired excuses. And if he has stopped drinking, why not pick it up where he left off? Thus, whether to drink or not is a never-ending contest between a natural good (health, family, etc.) and another natural good (the pleasures of alcohol—ignoring for the moment its dark side). But in this contest of competing goods, the one that offers *immediate* gratification—alcohol—too often wins out.

With the Matt Talbot Way, however, the contest is put on a higher plane, or more precisely on a tilted playing field—one on which the old natural good is at a distinct disadvantage. Indeed, the old contest, the constant tug of war, becomes no contest at all. While you may use the same natural reasons—loss of job, family, health, etc.—to prod you to the point of deciding that you've got to begin following the Way, the motivation needed to actually follow through and quit is of the *supernatural* order—the love of God. This all-important difference is what gives the Matt Talbot Way its power, its unique advantage over other methods of attaining and maintaining sobriety. The difference may not be apparent at the outset—and probably incomprehensible to someone looking for a completely secular approach, such as Rational Recovery—but as you proceed along the Way, you will slowly begin to savor your newfound power and to understand how you were able to develop it.

It now becomes difficult, if not impossible, for you to identify with your old life, your old self. No longer will you be dependent on alcohol or any group in its place. Alcohol no longer has power over you. You won't realize this immediately upon giving up drink—you will be too amazed that you have been able to quit to think much about anything else. But after a time of sober reflection, the deeper nature of what has happened will begin to dawn upon you.

Chapter IV

An Appeal to the Heart

During the Passion, Peter three times denied knowing Jesus. When Jesus confronted him after his Resurrection, he did not charge him with his weakness or his failings. But he did want to know whether he loved him. Three times he asked the same question, "Do you love me?" An exasperated Peter answered each time, "Lord, you know I love you" (John 21:15-17).

So it is for the follower of the Matt Talbot Way. You are called to follow Peter's example as Jesus asks you the same question: "Do you love me?" Jesus waits to hear you say, "Lord, you know I love you." Once you become armed with that love, you will be able to make a completely free, unconditional gift of the pleasures of drink—you will quit drinking for love of Jesus Christ.

Like a child, you may think of your gift as coming solely from yourself, though of course your capacity to make such a gift comes from God. And like a child you go about preparing your gift "in secret," as though God didn't even know about it. Only by an act of your will can you choose to love him—he won't force you to. And only by an act of your will can you make your uncommon gift of love.

To be able to do this you must pray regularly and in a definite fashion. By itself, the most heartfelt resolution to quit drinking won't do. You must pray systematically to develop the depth of love on which everything else depends.

Too often Christians approach God as though he were a monkey on a chain, and they, the organ grinder: Just say the right prayers, give a few yanks on the chain, and God will dance to their tune. And God help Him if He doesn't dance the right jig. After all, they are "good" Christians: if only they pray with enough fervor, God will surely do their bidding. But when God does not seem to catch the tune, and things don't turn out their way, they begin to lose heart. They wonder whether he really cares enough to listen, or whether anyone is even there to listen. Rather than their faith being strengthened, it becomes fragile, ready to be shattered from the least stress. Too often they lose whatever faith they have and end up worshiping strange gods.

We tend to be unwilling to take God on his own terms. We decide what is best for him to do, and then we pray for that. But God is responsive to our needs, not necessarily our wants. Although it is natural to tell him of those needs, we should not dictate precisely how they should be met. If our prayers are to be truly effective—that is, pleasing to God—we should dispose ourselves to accept whatever he sends us. We must learn to substitute his will for our own: Thy will be done. We hope that he will "hear" our prayers, but it is more important that we hear and accept what he has in mind for us.

All prayer should express our love and adoration for God. Even when we pray for worldly benefits, we implicitly recognize that he is the source of all good. Although praying for things may not be the perfect way to pray, it still expresses our dependence on him. But even when we pray for something we need, we should pray as though everything depends on God, and then act as though it's all up to us.

The most perfect forms of prayer are those of adoration, praise, thanksgiving and love. True love expects nothing in return: it forgets itself. We love God because the object of our love is deserving of our unreserved love. Although this may seem an unrealistically pure stance to take, it is exactly how you, as a follower of the Matt Talbot Way, must pray. You pray that your love for God, particularly in the person of Jesus Christ, will grow "without measure." Your objective is to come to love him with an ever increasing love, with nothing being asked for or expected in return. Of course you do have an ulterior motive—at least at the outset: You know that if you can love him more than drink, you will be able to make a pure gift to him of its comforts and pleasures. You will be able to stop drinking.

Continued sobriety, however, as the primary objective of the Way will tend to fade further and further into the background as you proceed. The reason for being of Matt's Way, and why you will continue to follow it, is that it has become the sure means to grow in love for God. Love of God will have become the primary objective of the Way, with sobriety reduced to being merely a pleasant side effect. Your prayers of love and adoration will have become perfect because you expect absolutely nothing in return, even though in the back of your mind you know that if you ever stopped following the Way you would surely return to drinking.

If love for Jesus Christ is the driving force behind the Way, you need to have a clear idea of his true nature. What is so lovable about him that you should be willing to give up the delights of alcohol? Since you propose to do without part of God's creation, what is the nature of that creation? Is the world and all that's in it good? Or is part of it evil? Where does alcohol fit into the scheme of things? Can it really be good? Is it fitting that it should be made a gift to God?

Everything created by God is good. What man does with his creation is another matter. C.S. Lewis has written that "It is the stealing of the apple that is bad, not the sweetness. The sweetness is still a beam from glory.... There is sacrilege in the theft. We have abused a holy thing."[1] In the same way, you may have abused drink—this "holy thing"—but its essential goodness remains unsullied.

The Bible is full of approving comments about wine, summed up by the Psalmist who speaks of how it will "gladden the heart of man" (Psalms 104:15). But for every approval there are cautions that it be used in moderation, with drunkenness being condemned outright.

Jesus had an easygoing attitude towards wine, without even a hint of shame when he and his disciples drank it. Quite the contrary: There were many occasions when he and his friends enjoyed themselves as they ate and drank together. When he was accused of being "a glutton and a drunkard," and compared unfavorably with John the Baptist, who ate little and drank nothing, he didn't even bother to refute the exaggerations (Luke 7:33).

Jesus performed his first miracle at the marriage feast of Cana by changing water into wine only after the guests had "drunk freely" and the wine had run out. He was not against people having a good time. He had no problem with the possibility—even probability—that his miracle might be the means for some of the guests to drink too much: apparently many of them had already had plenty when his mother pointed out to him that there was no more wine (John 2:1-11). And at the Last Supper, it was through the means of bread and wine that Jesus chose to express his continuing love for his followers.

The point in all this is that there is no reason to question the fitness of a gift to God of the pleasures of drink. This is true regardless of how much you have misused it in the past. If there has been sin, it has come from within you and not from the drink. Alcohol given up solely for love of Jesus always remains a pure gift of love. And because it is a gift of part of the best of God's creation, not only is it acceptable to him, it is always lovingly, even eagerly, received as something that truly comes from the heart.

But why give up drink in the first place? You know from sad experience the suffering your drinking can cause those around you whom you are supposed to love; that by itself should be enough reason to make you stop. But your selfishness when it comes to drink overwhelms whatever considerations you have for others. Only through a more demanding love can you overcome your love of alcohol. Only in God—particularly in the person of Jesus Christ—do you find that something or someone able to draw from you a far greater love.

So, Jesus is the key to the Matt Talbot Way. For the Way to begin to make sense to you, you must understand not just who he is, but precisely *what* he is. Is he wholly God? wholly man? co-equally God and man? or something in between? Unless you get his *nature* straight, you will never be able to develop the kind of love for him on which the way depends so completely. You have got to know what sort of person he really is if you are going to be able to develop the underlying motivation needed to quit drinking the Matt Talbot Way.

Jesus put the question directly to his disciples: "Who do men say that I am?" Was he just a man with a keenly developed moral insight, who had a way of tossing off pithy sayings that delighted his followers but provoked the authorities to kill him? If he was only a man, he was either a madman, a fool, or an imposter, considering the extraordinary claims he made for himself. No wonder he was crucified—indeed, a strong case can be made that he brought it on himself. If he was only a man, though, even if we ignore what must have been the lies he told about himself and accept him simply as a great moral teacher—someone on the order of a Socrates or a Gandhi—it is preposterous to think that Matt Talbot or anyone else would be willing to give up drink simply for love of such a man. One would have to be a complete fool to be so enchanted by a mere man, charming though he may have been.

The whole point behind Christianity is that because of man's sinful and fallen nature, his fitness for union with God had to be perfected: he had to become reconciled with God. To heal the breach required an atonement that only God could bring about. Man could not set things straight on his own. From all eternity the Second Person of the Trinity—the Son of God—possessed the nature of God in all its fullness. If the Son took on the human nature of fallen man as well, a life lived in perfect obedience to the Father would meet the test.

In time the Son was sent on such a mission, coming into the world as Jesus, the son of Mary and Joseph. The person of Jesus was God, the Second Person of the Trinity, in all his divinity, but at the same time he had a fully developed human nature. Any action of Jesus had two natures that he could draw upon. But whatever he did, it was always the single person of Jesus who did it, and that person was God. The stage was now set for the salvation of mankind to be worked in a perfect fashion.

Jesus was a gift from God to help make men worthy to be reunited with God. He did this by living a just life in obedience to his Father. He left it only after suffering an excruciatingly painful death on the cross. And he rose from the dead and now communicates that life to us so that we can live not a sinful and unjust life, but a new life in him, totally united to God.

That God would deign to become man has always astonished us. But we often have more difficulty in accepting the humanity of Jesus than his divinity. There is a strong tendency to think of him as God who hides behind a human face, with his manhood completely overwhelmed by his divine nature. If that were so, the one who suffered and died on the cross was no flesh-and-blood Jesus, but rather the mere appearance or shadow of a man. If his "human" faculties were worn only as a mask, his suffering and death would never convey the same awe and compassion as does the pain and death of the real God-man we know as Jesus Christ.

Jesus, although fully divine, had the same capacity to enjoy life and feel its pains as any of us. He willingly submitted to the pain and intense suffering of crucifixion for love of mankind—indeed, he lovingly took it on for each of us individually. It is this Jesus Christ—*in all his humanity*—you must come to love and admire in a special way if you are to be a follower of the Matt Talbot Way. It is not just that Jesus is God that motivates you to quit drinking—though divine justice by itself should be enough to make you quit. Rather, it is Jesus in his humanity, and the extreme fashion in which he emptied himself, which eventually drives you to do something special as a free expression of love for him.

Just as Jesus in obedience to his Father proved his love for us in an utterly convincing fashion by the unrestrained manner in which he poured out his life, so you, as a follower of the Matt Talbot Way, look for a way not just to speak of love, but to do something that will speak far louder and clearer than any words. Even at this late date, in a show of solidarity you stand at the foot of the cross with Mary, John, and the others and commiserate with the crucified Christ. But it is more than just a show. For love of him you choose to stand there without the pleasures and comfort of drink. Jesus in all his divinity may demand your adoration, but it is Jesus *in his humanity* to whom you pour out your love in a unique way.

Even now the human heart of the glorified Jesus is divinely responsive to followers of the Matt Talbot Way. Jesus understands in a keenly human way the cost of your gift of the pleasures of drink—your "little folly"—to the Father for love of him. God will not refuse you when you pray that your love for Jesus may grow "without measure."

Your act of giving up alcohol by itself may not have any value in God's sight, but as a pure expression of love for his Son that springs from your heart, it is irresistible to him. Since God himself is love, love is his vulnerable point; through love you are able to conquer him.

To reach this point as you follow the Matt Talbot Way, you must understand who you are, what you are, and where you fit into God's creation. For this you need to develop true humility. Being humble doesn't mean that you have to think little of yourself, grovel before people, or try to appear lowly in the eyes of the world. You can be humble even while honestly proud of the gifts with which God has endowed you. To be humble simply means that you have faced the truth about yourself and who God is, and you fully understand and admit your relationship to him as well as to your fellow creatures.

You must recognize that you are not only a creature but a child of God. And as a child, you must develop a childlike trust—an attitude of complete dependence on him. Jesus emphasized that "unless you turn and become like children you will never enter the kingdom of heaven" (Matthew 18:3). Jesus holds children out to us as models, not just because they are innocent, but because their nature is to love and expect love in return. As a child of God, you take delight in giving something special to him solely out of love. With Matt Talbot as your inspiration, you prepare your little gift "in secret"—as though God did not even know about it and as if it were completely your own doing. And because your gift is of love and comes from the heart, the heart of Jesus delights in receiving it.

Chapter V

An Uncommon Gift

Too much of any of the good things of the world makes life difficult, even miserable. If you are an alcoholic, eventually you have to face this inescapable truth. But you have within reach the power to turn the cause of your difficulties into a source of strength, and ultimately, into a means of attaining peace of mind and spirit. What has become your undoing can lead not only to a revitalized life, but to a completely new kind of life.

By following the Matt Talbot Way to sobriety, you are able to develop a motivation so powerful that you freely want to stop drinking for good. To do this, however, you must relearn how to be generous. Ordinarily, an alcoholic is inclined towards generosity—that is part of his problem: he is too liberal with himself and tends towards excess in all things. It is his love for alcohol that makes him push the rest of the world aside—even those he loves—as he keeps reaching for the bottle.

If you are to overcome yourself and your alcoholism, you must revitalize your innate generosity and direct it away from yourself. As a follower of the Matt Talbot Way, not only will you learn how to do this, but you will learn to do it in a perfect fashion. You will do it by making a complete gift of yourself, including all of your actions, to God each day. In particular, you offer him the pleasures and delights you find in alcohol, not by drinking and enjoying it as in the past, but by choosing to do without it as an express act of love for his Son Jesus Christ.

Your objective is to show your love for God in the most active and honest way of which you are capable. By focusing your love on him, you are able to develop a *positive* motivation so powerful that it overwhelms your love for drinking. Choosing not to drink becomes an act of love that you will renew daily for as long as you like alcohol—no doubt for the rest of your life.

When you quit the Matt Talbot Way, it won't be because you are afraid of losing something, whether it's your job, your family, your home, your health—all *negative* motivations, and all good reasons that alcoholics have relied upon to quit—even though some or all of these may apply to you. No doubt worldly concerns are what have brought you to the point of wanting to stop in the first place; but taking the next step—actually quitting, and quitting for good—is another matter. Like Matt Talbot, you must develop a counter-attraction so powerful that it overwhelms your love and desire for drink. Inspired by his example, you will forego the pleasures of drink solely for love of Jesus Christ. You won't beg God to keep you from drinking; no one—not even God—is going to do that. In the end, only you will decide whether you are going to drink or not.

When people pray for spiritual gifts, even for such things as the virtue of temperance, God has a way of answering indirectly. But because of the innate purity of your prayers as you pray the Matt Talbot Way—your sole objective being to grow in love for God—your prayers will be answered directly. God has no way of saying no; your prayers are irresistible to him because you are asking him for what he most wants you to have. Praying in this fashion, your love for him must increase. And you will find that you must express that increased love in the best way you know.

From your increased love springs the uncommon gift of the pleasures of drink. You freely choose to give up what you have become so fond of solely for love of Jesus Christ. Your generosity will have been perfected. From then on, each day becomes a new opportunity to express your love for him by continuing to give back to him this most delightful good.

It all sounds so simple, and in many ways it is. But far more is demanded of you than just to make a firm resolution with love of God in mind. It's not that easy. Whether or not you have stopped drinking when you begin to follow the Matt Talbot Way, you must steadfastly follow a regimen of daily prayer designed to increase your love for God, particularly in the person of Jesus Christ. You must commit yourself to a few prayers each day. No one else will know what you are up to—it is a completely private matter—though you may want to confide in your family and close friends. But you will make no show of it, no pious ostentation.

Except for a few minutes a day of reading the Scriptures and spiritual matters, it takes no time away from your other activities. You can pray privately while in the normal course of your daily rounds—while walking, jogging, driving a car, riding a bus or train. Regardless of how busy you may be, you will never be able to excuse yourself on the grounds that you don't have time for this sort of thing.

The model for your new spiritual life is Matt Talbot, of course. Not only was he a Catholic; he was an Irish Catholic of the late nineteenth, early twentieth century—a most Catholic sort of Catholic. The devotional sensibilities of Catholics differ from other Christians; Protestants are frequently uncomfortable with many Catholic practices, even in areas where there is essential agreement on underlying beliefs. And for that matter, many of today's Catholics are uneasy with some of these things. Consequently, in formulating the Matt Talbot Way, elements that might seem too Catholic for the taste of Protestants, Orthodox, and other non-Catholic Christians have been modified to make them compatible with their basic Christian faith, but without doing violence to Matt's essential spirit.

Chapter VI

The Matt Talbot Way

The Matt Talbot Way is a stratagem based upon love: By systematically working to increase your love for Jesus Christ, a time will come when you will be able to give up the pleasures of alcohol simply for love of him. To bring this about, your faith and love must grow. For this, you must follow in a regular and systematic fashion the seven steps of the Way every day.

The Seven Steps of the Way

To prepare yourself for that moment of grace, you need a plan of action—a systematic program of prayer and spiritual development. In a sense, you must "put on" Matt Talbot, who can be described most simply as someone who had a great love for Jesus Christ. You must model yourself after him spiritually as you prepare to give up alcohol for love of Christ. Precisely how you do this is laid out step by step. The Matt Talbot Way is inspired by what we know of Matt's spiritual practices, but without the sheer excess that he brought to everything. The nonessentials of his life have been laid aside—what remains captures his fundamental spirit.

There are seven steps that you must follow every day:
1. Daily Offering
2. Dedication of prayers of the day
3. Christ-centered prayer
4. Spiritual reading
5. Short prayers during the day
6. Evening prayer
7. Christian living

1. Daily Offering

Your main objective as you follow the Matt Talbot Way is to be able to make the Daily Offering. This prayer is similar to the traditional one that many Christians say each day—a gift to God of oneself, including all of the day's activities, both worldly and spiritual. They express their complete reliance on the providence of God by accepting whatever the day might bring, and then offering all this to him as a gift of love.

The Daily Offering of the Matt Talbot Way, however, goes further. Its unique feature is the gift you make to the Father of the pleasures and delights of alcohol that you forgo—a gift that you make as an act of love for his Son, Jesus Christ. You make this gift unconditional; you don't say, "I will love you, Lord, if only you will stop me from drinking." Only you, not God, will decide whether or not you will drink. It is you who will choose not to drink because of the power that has been set loose in you—a power flowing *directly* from your love of Christ. Not only will you make this gift daily, usually in the morning, but the expression of your gift becomes a continuing act of love throughout the day since you continuously choose to do without alcohol.

Each day now reinforces your new way of life. The daily gift of the pleasures of drink, coupled with prayer, becomes the source of your power to make the next day's gift. By giving of yourself in this fashion your love for God grows day by day: love now feeds on love. The possibility that one day you will suddenly become so bad-mannered and ungrateful as to demand the return of your gift, of what you had given so freely in the past, becomes unthinkable—at least as long as you continue to follow the Way.

Daily Offering

> Heavenly Father, being mindful of the heroic example of your servant Matt Talbot, I offer you during this day myself, all my works and prayers, joys and sorrows, and in particular, the worldly pleasures and delights of alcohol [or drugs or whatever else you are attached to but have decided to give up], which I forgo, as an expression of love for your Son, Jesus Christ. I pray that these gifts may be pleasing to you and that you will favor me with your blessing, through the same Christ, our Lord. Amen.

Although Matt Talbot is mentioned in the prayer, he is held up only for imitation, and then only in a limited way. You don't ask for his intercession with God to keep you from drinking. Furthermore, you don't take a "pledge" to stop drinking as Matt did. (When Matt quit, he made a pledge for three months, and then extended it several times before making it permanent.) Rather, each day becomes a new opportunity to show your love for God. Your gift is made in a sober-minded, down-to-earth fashion, not as some abstract declaration of love that could easily be lacking in sincerity. It must be genuine because what you give you have valued so highly. With a gift that must come from the heart, there is no possibility of a phony show of generosity.

The Daily Offering is best made immediately upon waking. It is the spiritual focal point of each day and gives purpose and direction to everything else. Although listed as the first step of the Way, it can be more precisely thought of as the final step—the climax of the day. More exactly, it is the culmination of the spiritual activities of all the previous days taken together, beginning from when you embarked on the Way. The point at which you will be able to take this first step depends entirely on regular and systematic prayer. You can't just wake up one morning with the memory of last night's excesses still pressing on your mind, finally decide that you have had enough of drink, and then resolve to give it up. It doesn't come that easily.

Your ability to give up drink the Matt Talbot Way will depend entirely on how much you really love God. Once you decide you want to do it this way, you will probably find that whatever love you have for him is lukewarm at best, considering the affection you have lavished on drink. And it is not only a matter of your love being listless; the faith that your love depends on will probably be weak and uncertain, too.

To develop the faith and love needed to make the Daily Offering a reality, you must follow the other steps. If you do this with a steady resolve, you will reach a point when your love of God will have grown sufficiently for you to give up drink solely for love of him. Until then, when making your Daily Offering you should omit the words "and in particular, the worldly pleasures and delights of alcohol, which I forgo."

2. CHRIST-CENTERED PRAYER

Christ-centered prayer is the key step, in conjunction with the third, in preparing you for the Daily Offering. Your objective is to pray and meditate on the person of Jesus in order to open your mind to him and to allow him to enter your heart. If your faith and love are weak to begin with, as will usually be the case, the process of conversion has nonetheless begun as you call upon him in prayer. If you systematically and regularly pray in this fashion, it is only a matter of time before your love will have grown to the point where you will be ready to perfect your Daily Offering: You will give up drink as the direct result of that increased love.

You have a great deal of flexibility in deciding what Christ-centered prayers to use. Until you find something more to your liking, you may want to settle on the Jesus Prayer:

"Lord Jesus Christ, Son of God, have mercy on me, a sinner."

The Jesus Prayer is probably the best and easiest prayer with which to begin, particularly if you are out of the habit of praying regularly. But that doesn't mean that you are forever wedded to it; there may be other Christ-centered prayers that you will come to prefer. Nevertheless, as you begin to follow the Way, you will probably find the Jesus Prayer to be more than satisfactory. For Catholic followers of the Way, several alternative Christ-centered ways of praying traditional to them are listed in Appendix II. Also, these are more attuned to Matt Talbot's actual practices.

The Jesus Prayer is based solely upon the Gospels. St. Luke tells of Bartimaeus, the blind man sitting by the side of the road as Jesus was passing by, who cried out, "Jesus, Son of David, have mercy on me," begging to be cured of his blindness (Luke 18:35-43). Again in Luke, Jesus teaches in the parable of the Pharisee and the tax collector that we should be humble when we pray: "God, be merciful to me, a sinner" (Luke 18:9-14). With "Son of David" changed to "Son of God," the two prayers are integrated into a single formula: Lord Jesus Christ, Son of God, have mercy on me, a sinner.

The Jesus Prayer has a long history going back to the early centuries of the Church. For the early Christians, particularly in the East, it was a way to pray without ceasing. Today it is especially well-known to Orthodox Christians; but many others say it repeatedly as a simple and direct way to raise their consciousness of Jesus.

As you repeatedly pray the Jesus Prayer, your mind should be directed to the single thought of the God-Man, Jesus Christ, both in his humanity and his divinity. You should say it from the heart slowly at least one hundred times each day. Particularly effective is the synchronization of the prayer with the natural rhythm of your breathing. There is no special magic to the precise number of times you say it. By praying it repeatedly, however, you express the extent of your commitment to Christ, and continually indicate your welcome to him. This requires a steady effort, a disciplined dedication to prayer. But it is easier to develop and maintain a sense of discipline if you attach a number to what you are intent on doing.

Some Christians may object that repetition of prayers is what Jesus had in mind when he said, "In praying do not heap up empty phrases as the Gentiles do; for they think that they will be heard for their many words" (Matthew 6:7). What Jesus was warning against was trying to impress God with the sheer number of words rather than the involvement of the mind and heart. Repetition of the words in this prayer is a way of constantly directing your mind and heart towards Jesus in faith and love. St. Paul wrote that he "would rather speak five words with my mind" than ten thousand words unknowingly (1 Corinthians 14: 19). The Jesus Prayer is only twelve words, but praying these few words repeatedly with a loving disposition is a simple and direct way to grow in love for Jesus Christ.

3. DEDICATION OF PRAYERS OF THE DAY

After saying the main body of your Christ-centered prayers, you should pray the following prayer:

Prayer to the Holy Spirit

O Holy Spirit, may I receive Jesus Christ into my heart through you. As Mary his mother did, may I learn to know and love him without measure as Lord and Savior. Draw me to him so I can imitate him in all things and thereby obtain the blessing of my heavenly Father, through the same Christ, our Lord. Amen.

This prayer gives purpose and direction to what you are trying to accomplish through the other steps. It expresses your general intention that as a result of *all* your prayers, your love for Jesus Christ may grow "without measure." You don't ask God to keep you from drinking or even for the virtue of temperance; rather, you pray solely that your love for him may increase—particularly for the person of Jesus Christ. (Nevertheless, there will probably be times—moments of weakness or crisis, both before and after you stop drinking—when you will appeal directly to him for immediate help in not drinking.)

As your love grows, there will come a time when you will be able, solely for love of Jesus, to give back to God what you have become so fond of. In getting there, you will go about preparing your gift to God "in secret." Though you may think of it as coming solely from you, your capacity to make such a gift comes from God, of course. Ultimately, though, it is through your own will power—power springing from your love of Christ—that you will be able to quit drinking.

In place of the Prayer to the Holy Spirit, followers of the Way who are not only Christians, but Catholics, will probably want to substitute the following prayer, though either version may be used:

An Appeal to the Mother of God

> O Blessed Mother of God, I beg you that I may receive your Son, Jesus, into my heart, through the Holy Spirit by whom you conceived him. Teach me to know and love him without measure, as you adore him as Lord and Savior. Draw me to him so that I may imitate him in all things and thereby obtain the blessing of our heavenly Father, through the same Christ, our Lord. Amen.[1]

Recast in this manner, the prayer more closely reflects the thinking and attitude of Matt Talbot as he prayed and grew in love for Jesus. Matt asked for Mary's help in this task; he knew that she wanted this above all for him. Also, the prayer is more attuned to the devotion that Catholics have towards Mary, whom they look upon not only as the mother of Jesus but their spiritual mother as well.

4. Spiritual reading

Through prayer you will be able to develop your love of God to the point where it acts as a counter-attraction to your fondness for drink. Love comes from the heart, but the heart needs to be stimulated by the mind. Not only must you begin to know what it is you must love, but you must constantly increase your knowledge of it. As you begin to follow the Way, your faith, as well as your love of God, will probably be weak. Both of these depend to a certain degree on a basic knowledge of God and spiritual matters. If you are to grow spiritually, you must systematically build a foundation of knowledge to nourish your faith and ultimately your prayers.

To broaden your knowledge you must spend fifteen minutes or so each day reading spiritual matters. This is the only part of the Matt Talbot Way that makes any demand on your time. When you think back to all the time you have wasted in drinking and then sobering up, you should have no trouble in finding these few minutes. A good time is just before going to bed.

The foundation of your reading should be the Bible, particularly the New Testament. You must learn more about what sort of man Jesus is, and then cultivate a strong admiration for him as a person. Only if you get to know him well will you be able to develop the love upon which the Matt Talbot Way depends. Besides reading the Bible, lives of Christ and the like, you should read other books that increase your faith and knowledge of spiritual matters in a general way.

5. Short Prayers During the Day

We tend to take the good things of the world for granted, as though they didn't come from God. To overcome this natural insensitivity, you should look for ways to remind yourself that God is your Creator, you are his creature, and all good things of life depend upon him. Grace before meals is a simple reminder of that essential relationship.

Outside of mealtime you should become more responsive in expressing your appreciation in other ways. Open yourself up to a few occasions each day of spontaneously sending a passing shaft of prayer in thanksgiving for life's little pleasures. You only have to look around to see God's love expressed in all things.

By becoming more attuned to God's loving concern in little things, you will begin to understand in some small measure the extent of his generosity—that the Son of God died on the cross for love for you. And you will become better able to respond to that generosity in your own fashion—you will offer to him the delights of drink as a gift of love.

Christ-centered prayers of Step Two, such as the Jesus Prayer (and for Catholics, the Rosary or Mass), are key to the Matt Talbot Way; but you should look beyond them for other occasions to round out your prayers during the day. Catholics, for example, may want to silently pray the Angelus about midday, and the Prayer to the Crucified Christ (see Appendix II) at about three o'clock in the afternoon in daily remembrance of the crucifixion of Jesus.

6. Evening prayer

Evening prayer is the natural culmination of the spiritual activities of the day. You have complete freedom in selecting prayers that you are most comfortable with. You may keep them as brief as you wish. This is a good time to rededicate all of the day's prayers to your primary objective of growing in love for Jesus Christ. Here is an excellent evening prayer:

The Canticle of Simeon (The Nunc Dimittis)
>Now, Master, you may let your servant go in peace,
>according to your word,
>for my eyes have seen your salvation,
>which you have prepared in sight of all the peoples,
>a light for revelation to the Gentiles,
>and glory for your people Israel.
>Glory be to the Father,
>and to the Son,
>and to the Holy Spirit,
>as it was in the beginning,
>is now, and ever will be, world without end.
>Protect us, Lord, as we stay awake; watch over us
>as we sleep: that awake, we may keep watch with
>Christ, and asleep, rest in his peace. Amen.

7. Christian living

An essential part of the Way is that followers adhere to generally recognized Christian norms of living. The demands of church and society must also be considered. It is the height of hypocrisy to make your Daily Offering upon awakening, and then to live like a heathen the rest of the day, even though you say a few prayers. You are not expected to be perfect, but you must at least dispose yourself to trying to lead a Christian life. But even here, if you should find yourself seemingly locked into a moral predicament (other than drinking) outside of these norms, don't despair of being able to overcome your alcoholism the Matt Talbot Way. Although you may not have that same assurance of success you otherwise would, still, by resolutely following the Way, you may wind up overcoming not only your alcoholism but the other as well.

Chapter VII

GETTING STARTED

WHEN AN ALCOHOLIC FIRST BEGINS TO DRINK, HE IS DELIGHTED WITH his new sense of power. He finds that he can raise his spirits at will—a few drinks and the genie is set loose from the bottle to work its magic. Only later does he realize that the genie has turned on him as it begins to make increasingly outrageous demands that he can't seem to refuse. He finds that he has no defense against its lures: unable to leave it alone, unable to quit on his own.

As you begin to follow the Matt Talbot Way in earnest, you will make a far more significant discovery. You will find something akin to bootstrap power to draw upon in overcoming your addiction. Once you learn how to tap into it and use it against your fickle friend the bottle, drink will no longer have any sway over you.

Essential to the Matt Talbot Way is your faith, even though you may be Christian in little more than name. Patterns of excessive drinking may have left little room for the active practice of it. And even as a system of belief, it may be little more than a set of hazy remembrances from childhood. Yet presumably there remains a remnant of faith, a spark that can ignite your hope and expectation at least to the possibility that the Way will work for you.

As you approach the Matt Talbot Way, you may only want to be able to quit drinking without too much trouble. The idea of becoming serious about Christianity may not be what you had in mind. Still, you know you have to do something to get the upper hand over drink; after the Matt Talbot Way has served its purpose, maybe you can just put it aside and forget it.

So, you find yourself in a box—a box of your own making, perhaps, but a box nonetheless. What have you got to lose? You decide if you must do something, why not do it the Matt Talbot Way—all nice and easy.

But the Way demands a lot more commitment than that. Nevertheless, you should not worry about this at the outset. The long-term role that you think Jesus Christ ought to play in your life is something you can decide later on. Although there is no need for conversion in the usual sense, since presumably you are already a Christian, nonetheless there must be a conversion of the heart. You must turn towards Jesus Christ. And as part of that turning, eventually you will choose to give up the pleasures of drink solely for love of him.

But don't think that this is some sort of soppy, sentimental love. Rather, the love and friendship you must develop is much the same as that which his disciples had for him. They were rough, commonplace people who came from the lower end of society. For two or three years they tramped the countryside with their teacher, eating, drinking, and sleeping as the closest of friends. From this tight camaraderie it would have been only natural for them to have become quite fond of him, even if he had only been a rather average person—simply a nice guy. They listened and learned from this man whom the Gospels portray as a most lovable sort of person. He said wonderful things about himself and his kingdom, and he performed miracles, both on the body and the spirit. And they came to believe he was the long-awaited Messiah.

Then he was suddenly taken from them and crucified; but he rose from the dead after three days. Even so, his disciples did not fully understand who he was until the coming of the Holy Spirit at Pentecost. One thing is certain, though: This uneducated, unfashionable band of followers had a deeply felt love for him, both as to the man they knew as teacher and friend, as well as the Savior and Son of God they came to know. Anyone who calls himself a Christian should have no difficulty in emulating them and the unreserved love and friendship they had for him. If you are contemplating following the Matt Talbot Way, the idea of giving up alcohol for the love of such a person should in no way be seen as a maudlin, bleeding-heart display that people naturally shrink from.

Although a generalized desire to quit drinking may get you to thinking about doing it the Matt Talbot Way, actually following through demands much more. You may see the wisdom of pursuing it, but you do not yet have sufficient motivation to say no to alcohol for good.

As long as you love it more than Christ, you will continue to drink; when you begin to love him more than drink, you will be able to quit—it is as simple as that. In getting to that point, your first step must be at least to see it as your goal. That you are beginning to think about it, and even to like the idea, no matter how weak and imperfect your desire seems to be, indicates that it has become more than a mere possibility.

The Matt Talbot Way contains all that you need to take those difficult, first steps. Although you may be ready to quit drinking immediately, more often than not, you won't. During these early days as your love for Christ is growing, the only difference between the program you follow then, and what you will do later, is that for the time being, it may be that you will continue to drink even as you follow it in all other respects. If this should be your situation, when you make your Morning Offering, omit the words, "and in particular, the worldly pleasures and delights of alcohol, which I forgo." Even though you continue to drink, however, you are generating within yourself, through your increasing love for Christ, the means to quit.

A time will come—a moment of grace—when your conversion to Christ will be ready to be perfected. Your love for him will have grown to the point where it will outweigh your attachment to alcohol. Then it will become clear that you must express that love by the gift to God of what you hold so dear. You will give up the pleasures of drink solely for love of him. You will quit drinking, not because of the harm drink does to you and those around you, but because this has become the perfect way for you to show your love for Christ.

Matt Talbot's moment of grace came one Saturday after having spent over half his life pursuing drink with that thoroughness known so well to the alcoholic. When refused a few drinks by his companions, he decided that he had had enough. His friends had failed him—now he would turn to Christ. But his friends' callousness itself was not the cause of his moment of grace; it was simply the handy circumstance he used to prod himself to perfect his gift. In the same way, an outside event—such as, pressure from your family and employer—will not be the cause of your moment of grace. But it can be the means you use to move yourself to the point where you finally decide to make complete your proposed gift to God. As a result of that decision, you will give up drink for good for love of Christ.

Love is the driving force of the Way, the source of its power. But faith is what that love must feed on. Prayer is simply an expression of faith, and the faith of Christians becomes vital and animated only if they pray. But what if your faith is weak to begin with? What if you think you don't even have enough faith to say the prayers of the Way? You must nonetheless pray as best you can, even if you do not feel like it. You must make yourself want to pray. Simply *begin*, even if your prayers seem mechanical and lifeless at first.

If you *want* to pray, even though at first it seems that you cannot, you are actually opening yourself to the possibility of faith—that is all the crack that is needed. "Lord, I believe; help my unbelief!" The moment you decide that you want to believe, that you want to pray, you are able to pray—in fact, you *are* praying. From that fragile beginning will spring a flowering of faith if you actively nourish it; the love of God which depends on that faith will blossom with it. And the best nourishment to your growing faith is simply more prayer. By persevering and submitting to the disciplined prayer of the Way, your faith and love will grow and eventually culminate in the gift to God of the pleasure you find in alcohol.

Your prayers as you follow the Way are not the usual prayers of petition, asking for some worldly good, or even a spiritual good, such as the virtue of temperance. Rather, they are directed towards asking only that your love for Jesus Christ may increase "without measure." In this way your prayers become irresistible to God—they will always be answered precisely as you have fashioned them because you are asking for the one thing he most wants you to have.

God will not force you to love him, and you can't quit all by yourself. But you do have the capacity—in cooperation with the Holy Spirit—to love him. You must use that capacity by exercising your will to move towards him in love. Or more correctly, you must respond to the invitation of the Holy Spirit, which has been there all along, to love him. By doing this you become, in effect, a co-creator with the Creator: A measure of yourself comes into being that did not exist before, the creation of which required the action of both you and God. From this springs your newfound power over alcohol. Through your increased love of Jesus Christ you are able to give up the pleasures of drink.

Before your love of Christ can increase to that point, however, you need to get to know him better. You can't really love someone about whom you know little. To find out about the real Jesus, you must go to the historical sources that tell about him. Your objective should not be just to learn about Jesus, but to come to know him in a Christian sense—to know him in such a way that it transforms your life. By increasing your knowledge of him, you will develop a strong admiration for him as a person. From this increased knowledge and admiration, in combination with prayer, you will evolve a greater love for him. The power generated by this love is the same power you will ultimately draw on to quit drinking. For this reason, it is essential that you spend about fifteen minutes every day in spiritual reading.

If you are to develop an image of him that is faithful to the real Jesus, one that will draw you to him in the same way that his disciples were drawn to him, you must read the Gospels. Here, you will get to know and admire him as a living person. By reading them with faith, the dry bones of the text will begin to be clothed with the flesh of the real Jesus.

Even if you think that you know the Gospels, you should approach them as though you had never read them before. Indeed, you should read them as though you had never even heard of Jesus. And you should read them again and again. As the various Gospel scenes pass before your mind's eye, you should dispose yourself to listen to his words as though you were in the crowd following him, as though you were a bystander as he spoke to his disciples and the others. As you ponder these scenes, you will begin to realize that they were not meant to be just a private viewing for a few followers some two thousand years ago. You will hear his words as though you had actually been there, as though he was talking to you—which, of course, he was.

To begin your spiritual reading, you will need a copy of the Bible. It should be understood, however, that the Gospels were not meant to be a history of Jesus as we ordinarily understand the word. To a certain degree they are theological statements about the risen Christ made by a few men of faith for many other people of faith. To get a lively sense of the flesh-and-blood Jesus, as well as to see the four Gospels as parts of a single, continuous story, you should read at least one good Life of Christ, one that integrates the four Gospels with the details of the Jewish and Roman world of his time.[1] While such lives may not be completely satisfactory from an historical point of view, nevertheless they can provide you with a keen sense of the living and risen Jesus.

You will also do well to read a few books on spiritual development, particularly those that emphasize cultivating a strong personal admiration for Jesus. Here again, your objective is not so much to learn more about the historical Jesus who has lived and is no longer, as it is to come to know the Jesus who has lived and still lives.

As you read the New Testament, you will see that the disciples were slow to understand who Jesus really was. His disciples didn't begin to understand until after his Resurrection and the coming of the Holy Spirit at Pentecost—but understand they eventually did. So, too, you will begin not only to know the real Jesus—man and God—but to believe in him in a more vital way.

Jesus will emerge from your spiritual reading not only as Lord and Savior, but as an utterly lovable person—someone who now lives and demands a response from you. You respond on one level by believing in him; but if your faith is to be a living faith, it demands your love as well, unless it is to be nothing more than a hypocritical pose.

Love has a way of making its own demands; it must express itself. As a follower of the Way, you have set yourself to imitating the example of Matt Talbot. Like Matt, you have been preparing "in secret" for that moment of grace when you will finally make your own unique gift of love for the crucified and risen Christ.

Your moment of grace may come almost immediately after you decide that you want to follow the Matt Talbot Way, and you do in fact begin to follow the Way. But quite possibly the end to your drinking may not follow that quickly. You may think you are unworthy to receive the spiritual gifts you pray for. There is a natural tendency to become discouraged, but you should remember that Jesus taught that we "ought always to pray and not lose heart" (Luke 18:1). As you proceed along the Way, keep your mind on your objective of growing in love for Christ.

But you may doubt whether love for Christ by itself will ever be enough to make you give up what you have come to love so well. Worse, you may question whether you really want to give it up just for love of him. There is only one prescription for this: You must continue to follow the steps of the Way more resolutely and faithfully. At times you may feel as though you are making no headway, but the mere fact you choose to continue means you are succeeding. If you just persevere, it is only a matter of time before you reach your goal.

As you continue on your Way, a time will come when you hear, in a sense, Jesus' question, "Do you love me?" When that happens—when your moment of grace arrives—you will answer as Peter did: "Yes, Lord; you know that I love You." You will then find yourself compelled to give up the pleasures and delights of drink as an act of love for him. This will be the surest and best way, at least for you, to show that you do indeed love him.

In time, Matt Talbot may be canonized by the Catholic Church as St. Matt. If so, it will not be just because he gave up drink, but rather for the perfection of his life afterwards. But that new life would never have been possible if he had not stopped drinking. His moment of grace was not only the turning point of his life, it may well have been the spiritual high point. It is not too bold to conjecture that quite possibly, even probably, your moment of grace, when it comes, will be viewed with no less favor by God, considering the tremendous resolve and commitment required as you move towards Christ and away from drink. But once you do in fact follow through and quit, don't let yourself become self-satisfied, as though it all depended on you. To be sure, you will have taken power for yourself—a roundabout stratagem based on love of God. Rather than passively praying to him to make and keep you sober, you have reached out and taken what he had been offering you all along. Just don't forget that it was his love and generosity which were there in the first place that made it possible.

Chapter VIII

Markings Along the Way

It isn't easy to commit yourself to regular prayer. But because the routine of the Matt Talbot Way is fixed, you avoid the uneasiness or even outright anxiety that tends to develop when taking a more casual approach. Spontaneity in prayer is good but usually it is not there when you need it. By following a set program, you don't worry about the originality of your prayers or what comes next. With a familiar and comfortable track before you, you always know where you are going and how to get there.

Prayer is more than reciting a few prescribed words, of course: the essential element is the lifting of mind and heart to God. Don't worry that conditions aren't always ideal to pray—simply begin. If you have to choose between praying now, even though you don't seem to be able to give it your total commitment, and not praying at all as you wait for an ideal period of peace and quite—which may not come—always choose to pray now. Although your prayers may be imperfect (as most are), the fact that you are praying indicates that you really want to move towards God, even if that movement is erratic at times.

Most people are only too ready with excuses when confronted with the need to pray. Everyone seems to be busy, of course. But can you honestly claim that you don't have the time? The only demand that the Matt Talbot Way makes upon it is the fifteen minutes or so each day spent in spiritual reading. You should have little trouble in carving out such a small slice of time, considering how much you have wasted in past drinking. Besides, if you are like everyone else, you probably look for ways to waste time.

Except for spiritual reading, the various steps can be taken while you make your daily rounds. Waking up in the morning, showering, going for a morning jog, driving a car, riding a bus or train, walking to work, waiting in line—all easily lend themselves to the simultaneous performance of bits and pieces of the Way. With a little persistent effort, the whole thing is accomplished.

Some routine activities, however, are too involving at times to permit you to dispose yourself for the inner calm needed for prayer. For example, the mechanical demands of driving a car on the open highway are simple enough so that it is easy to put yourself on automatic pilot and retire into your inner chamber as you pray; but trying to do this in heavy traffic is neither safe driving nor effective prayer.

You have to use common sense about what works. No matter how busy you may be, though, you should always be able to find fifteen minutes or so of repeated, mechanical activities that permit you to pray without disturbing the rest of your day. Of course, it is all right to pray during a quiet time during the day if that is what you prefer and you can arrange it. The point about integrating prayer with the activities of the day is that once you understand how easily it is done, you will never have the excuse of not having enough time to pray.

Because the various steps of the Way are easily woven into the fabric of daily life, they can be performed without anyone realizing what you are up to. Friends and acquaintances may be amazed that you have suddenly given up drink, but there will be nothing in your daily activities to suggest how or why. Your life of prayer can be kept completely private with no outward show. Only a spouse need know anything—the pattern of spiritual reading will have become apparent. This is not to suggest that your family and friends must not find out; rather, whatever they do come to know will be because you choose to tell them.

Although the steps of the Way are essentially easy to perform, they are demanding in their own way. Before you begin to follow them, you may have been preoccupied with your drinking—planning for the next major or minor bout may never have been very far from your consciousness. When you begin to follow the Way, however, you will do so because it leads you to Jesus Christ and away from drink. (After you have been following the Way for awhile, you will probably find that your whole purpose in doing so is to grow in love for Christ—sobriety will have become simply a pleasant side effect.) The prior claim the Way makes upon whatever you will be doing that day will never be too far from your mind. Maintaining this new single-minded purpose, day after day, is not easy, at least at first.

You do not bind yourself to a set of rules, however, but you do dedicate yourself to Christ. Each day becomes another opportunity to renew your dedication by continuing to follow the steps of the Way. But you should not make the mistake of thinking you have made some sort of solemn vow; you have not taken a pledge to do or not do something (though Matt Talbot took a pledge at the outset). Rather, out of love you dedicate yourself to Christ. Once that love takes possession of you, you will find that you are willing to give up the enjoyment of alcohol solely as an expression of that love.

Because love is your underlying motivation, you leave no

room for fear of failure to become part of what drives you. Should you become fearful, the observance of the various steps of the Way would become mere obsessive compulsions. The vitality of your prayers would be sapped and the sought-after growth in love for Christ would be checked.

Once you begin to follow the Matt Talbot Way in earnest you will be unable to conceive of ever going back. Unlike the decision of members of A.A. to stay sober "One day at a time," your commitment extends as far into the future as you can envision. Through your prayers and your daily gift of the pleasures of drink, your love for Christ grows day by day. With each new day there is never any question whether you will continue on the Way; each day now becomes a new opportunity to express your devotion to Christ. The memory of your old drinking days recedes further and further into a hazy, distant past, as though those days belong to another life, which, of course, they do.

As you follow the steps of the Way, you may find that minor problems tend to develop. Some of these can be overcome with a little effort, others solved by making minor adjustments, and there are those that can simply be ignored. In no event, however, should you let yourself be seduced into thinking that some of the steps are not too important and can be skipped, even for a short time. By firmly setting aside fifteen minutes each day (though not necessarily in a single period) in which you blot out the world around you as best you can, you show a very real intention to pursue the love of God.

No doubt you would like to be able to sail through your prayers with your mind and imagination kept under tight control, but there will often be distractions. Keep in mind, though, that wanting to pray is at the heart of prayer; without it, prayer has little value. If you want to pray, your prayer retains its essence as prayer even though at times it seems that you are not praying at all. Your imagination may flit from one thing to the next, making it difficult to concentrate. But each time you overcome a distraction as you pray, you are indicating by an act of your will that you want to move towards God. Each of these little acts now becomes a new expression of love for God. Thus, distractions don't necessarily mean that your prayers are not effective. Quite the contrary: properly handled, they can become the means to increase the effectiveness of your prayers.

One way to overcome distractions is to turn them into the subject of your prayer. If someone intrudes into your prayers, pray for them briefly; if something bothers you, meditate upon it for a moment in prayerful fashion. Thus, whatever takes your mind off God becomes the link leading you back to him. But if your mind wanders aimlessly, or if you find yourself daydreaming, you should resist as best you can.

The petty worries of the day are among the biggest distractions. Give them no quarter; overpower them by driving them out of your mind. You will have plenty of time later, after the basic steps of the way have been taken care of, to give them all the attention they need. Real anxieties brought on by the force of events are a different matter. Depending on the extent of the problem, it may become difficult, if not almost impossible, to pray for any extended period of time. Still, do the best you can. But if anxieties do overtake you temporarily, don't become alarmed and think that you are failing to observe the way.

If praying makes you feel good, all well and good; but if you find you don't feel like praying or it leaves you with a sense of dryness, don't worry about it. What is important is not how it makes you feel, but rather that by an act of your will you are turning towards God.

Good feelings come and go, but if you come to depend on them, you may be seduced into thinking that without them you are not really praying. Effective prayer depends more on fidelity to the act of praying than to any good feelings it may bring about. The depth of your feelings, the vividness of your imagination or the originality of your thoughts are of little concern to God. What God wants is your loving commitment to move towards him—no matter how imperfect your prayers may seem at times. Your concern should be only with how well you dispose yourself to Christ's coming into your life.

If you are tired when you begin to pray, you will find it difficult to continue—prayer only adds to your fatigue. This shows the good sense of attending to the steps of the Way as early in the day as possible. The first step (the Daily Offering) should be taken as early as possible. And steps two and three—the heart of the Way—should not be left to the end of the day with the thought that somehow they can be worked in. Put them first on your agenda and take care of them as early as possible. If you should be ill on a particular day, do what you can.

Forgetfulness will become a problem at times; again, this is best overcome if the various steps are observed early in the day. If you forget a particular step, however, don't worry about it too much. For example, if you forget step five (short prayers during the day) from time to time, just resolve to do better. But if you constantly forget the more important steps, particular the first three, your resolution to give up drink for love of Christ needs to be strengthened. What you need to do is to rededicate yourself to following the Way. You should pray with renewed determination that you may grow in love for Christ. Direct your spiritual reading more particularly towards him and the Gospels. Possibly you should read or reread a good Life of Christ as you grope your way towards him.

Be on guard against developing a scrupulous attitude that demands performance of the steps with an exacting, meticulous care—that if you don't do them just so, you really aren't doing them at all. Nothing could be further from the spirit of the Way: Sweet reasonableness should be the test at all times. The Way is meant to be your cheerful companion and guide, not some demanding judge always ready to pounce on you and condemn you for some real or imagined shortcoming. This is not to suggest that you should expect or demand little of yourself; rather, remember your humanity and that everything you do contains elements of imperfection. Christ accepts, even expects, these imperfections (other than sin, of course)—so should you.

Chapter IX

A New Life

The idea of giving up the tangible pleasures of drink for what may seem like a distant love for Jesus Christ may not strike you as a fair trade at first. Jesus may have a certain appeal, but he just doesn't have the immediacy, the comfort of that next drink. Besides, you may never have been that serious about your Christian faith. Except for your drinking problem, you never would have considered taking up the Matt Talbot Way. But once you decide to give it a chance, what have you got to lose?

After you begin to follow the Way in earnest, even if you haven't stopped drinking yet, your knowledge and love of Jesus Christ will gradually grow. It is from this increased love that eventually springs your power—indeed, your need—to stop drinking, and to stop permanently. But as you get closer to the point of actually doing so, you may become frightened by the prospect of life without liquor. Alcohol continues to have a strong psychological hold on you. You may think you have got to have the stuff to make you whole; that without it, you will never be able to cope with or enjoy life. Besides, something that good deserves to be enjoyed. Indeed, it may seem ludicrous to you—almost a crime against nature—to turn your back on one of God's most pleasant and comforting gifts, even if it does cause "problems" from time to time.

When you finally quit, though, and the reality of sobriety begins to set in, your fears and doubts quickly pass. Almost immediately follows a brief period of amazement and utter disbelief. You are surprised at how much easier it was than you had expected—if only you had known you wouldn't have resisted so long. You begin to see how enjoyable life can be without alcohol. Inner calm and peace take over from the old disorder and anxiety. No longer are you preoccupied with drink, always preparing for the next session, always protecting the supply, and in the process, tending to blot out other plans.

Now it is your old preoccupation with drink that is blotted out. You feel as though a heavy load has been taken off your back. You are finally free to get on with life and all its possibilities without constantly worrying that alcohol will get in the way. The anxiety and depression that always seemed to be there when you were not drinking become things of the distant past. Your selfishness and other unattractive traits largely disappear. In the main, these "defects of character," as A.A. calls them, were tied to your drinking: once you quit, they tend to vanish.

By following the Matt Talbot Way, you "put on the Lord Jesus Christ," as St. Paul would say. By regularly praying in a Christ-centered fashion you cannot help but begin to model yourself on him. This, of course, is what being a Christian should be about. It may not be a cure-all for "defects of character" that are part of your basic personality; nevertheless, you will be a better person—less demanding, less self-centered, more sensitive to the needs of others. Having learned to love God better, and knowing of God's love for you, you will see a little clearer how you fit into the scheme of things—who you are, where you are going, and how best to get there.

Although intensely spiritual, the Matt Talbot Way is no escape from the world. It would be a mistake to think that followers see everything in an otherworldly fashion, that the world you live in is less real, or that all life's problems require spiritual solutions. Quite the contrary: Although you may face life more serenely, this should not be mistaken for a lack of concern for everyday problems or that you have less ambition and drive as you confront the world and the future. Rather, because alcohol and its attendant problems no longer weigh you down, you can finally get on with life.

Although you know firsthand the problems that alcohol can cause, this is no reason for you to be a prohibitionist. If anything, you will probably be an advocate of alcohol when used in moderation. The company of your friends who do drink will not threaten you, though you may be a little envious of those who can drink. But you should avoid those social situations where drinking seems to be the only reason for being there. At times, you may wonder if alcohol is really worth it to some of your friends as it doesn't seem to take much before they begin to look a little foolish if not a lot worse. But you will keep this to yourself except for those special situations that call for a few well-chosen words from a friend. If the Matt Talbot Way has been your liberation, do not make the mistake of thinking that all alcoholics who are Christians are ready to embrace it just because you mention it to them.

Still, people will be amazed that you have quit. If you wish, at an appropriate time you may let them know how you did it, though in a quiet way without being pushy or haughty. But pick your audience and your words carefully. People have a natural distrust of anyone who proclaims his religious convictions too loudly, particularly as to something so deeply felt as the underlying motivation required of the Matt Talbot Way. It's one thing to profess your belief as a Christian, but it's quite another to trumpet your love for Jesus Christ. People will probably look upon you with a great deal of suspicion. To come across as a pompous bore, simply say: "I have been able to give up drink because I have learned to love Jesus Christ more than drink"—even though that is the essential truth. It's not a question of being embarrassed about how you quit; you simply have to be prudent in explaining it.

Once you quit, each new day becomes an opportunity to privately reaffirm your love for Christ. You will never forget the pleasures of drink, nor will you want to forget them. You will continue to see alcohol as one of God's most delightful gifts. Life will not become a tug-of-war in which you constantly have to choose whether to drink or not. Your continuing affection for alcohol only serves to intensify your love for Christ. Each day's doing without it requires an express act of love for him—a reaffirmation of the love which drove you to quit in the first place. And the very act of pouring out that love not only immediately replenishes it, but actually increases it. From this increased love springs your power, your need, to do the same tomorrow.

The Matt Talbot Way is no quick fix, of course. It is not just something to get you off drink, then to be put aside as some passing fancy. It must become a permanent and integral part of your life. Your moment of grace will not come as a torrid religious experience with a blinding flash that overwhelms you. Rather, you must make a cool, reasoned decision to quit drinking—at the insistent prodding of the Holy Spirit and your heart, to be sure.

At some point you will probably find that your sole reason for continuing to follow the Way is to express your love for Christ—sobriety itself will have become just a welcome side effect. It may take a little while before you reach this purity of purpose. In the meantime, don't worry about it or even think about it; it will come about on its own when you are ready.

The possibility that one day you might decide to take back your gift of love and return to drinking becomes inconceivable—at least so long as you continue to follow the Way in all other respects. In the back of your mind, though, you know that if you ever did stop submitting to its discipline, you would surely revert to your old ways.

Soon you will probably come to boast quietly to yourself that you have quit drinking for good. More than that, there may come a time when you no longer look upon yourself as an alcoholic. You will consider yourself cured, at least provisionally—that is, as long as you continue to follow the Way. This is in direct contrast and conflict with the attitude of A.A. and virtually all professionals in the field of alcoholism: Once an alcoholic, always an alcoholic. A.A. impresses upon its members that they should see themselves as being permanently powerless over alcohol, that any control over it comes from outside of themselves—just keep going to meetings, and God, their Higher Power, or A.A. itself, will keep them sober. As a follower of the Matt Talbot Way, however, in time you may come to see that if there is one thing in life that you now have power over, it is alcohol. To be sure, you must always recognize that the source of your power is your love for Jesus Christ. If there should ever come a time when you would be so foolish as to think that it comes solely from within you, and that the Matt Talbot Way had served its purpose of getting you to stop drinking and may now be cast off as excess baggage, almost certainly you will return to your old drinking habits—you will once again be an alcoholic.

Looking back you may begin to wonder whether God set you up for what has happened. Has God used the delights of drink to get you to move towards him when nothing else might have worked? You proved only too compliant and cooperative in seeing that the stage was fully set. Without your natural affection for drink and your willingness to dive into the bottle, would the rest have been possible?

As a result of your fondness for alcohol, God has had his way with you. Only because you were so ready and so willing to allow it to bring you low did you finally have to choose between it and him. You will continue to see it not only as a delightful good, but as something far more: Drink has become the astonishing means by which you have been captivated and captured by God.

During your drinking days you may have excused yourself with the thought that you were only trying to increase your sensitivity to the world around you, even as to things spiritual. The first couple of drinks always seemed to do the trick. Actually, there really was a spiritual element, but not the way you may have thought. While you were pursuing the delusions of drink, God was on your heels in hot pursuit. You had become like a rabbit dashing across the fields, turning and dodging as you tried to avoid the relentless Hound. Francis Thompson was himself a reformed opium addict when he wrote these lines from *The Hound of Heaven*:

> I fled Him, down the nights and down the days;
> I fled Him, down the arches of the years;

> I fled Him, down the labyrinthine ways
> Of my own mind: and in the midst of tears
> I hid from Him…

Has God, in his loving, crafty way, not set you up for capture in his own sweet way, in his own good time? By his letting you have your way with drink for awhile, you found yourself in a fix where your only escape was to submit in weariness to the Hound:

> Whom wilt thou find to love ignoble thee,
> Save Me, save only Me?…
> Ah, fondest, blindest, weakest,
> I am He Whom thou seekest!

Chapter X

Models for Imitation

Matt Talbot is the perfect model to follow in transforming your love of drink into love of God. For this reason he is mentioned in the Daily Offering prayer—"being mindful of the heroic example of your servant Matt Talbot...." His example is positive proof of what you can do once you commit yourself in earnest to following the Matt Talbot Way.

In many ways, however, the preeminent model for a follower of the Matt Talbot way is Mary, the mother of Jesus. Although some Christians object to Catholic devotion to Mary (particularly as it may have been expressed in the past), considering it a needless interposition of a creature between man and God, there should be no question as to her role in the Matt Talbot Way. In the Prayer to the Holy Spirit, she is held up *only for imitation*: "Even as Mary his mother did, may I learn to know and love him without measure as Lord and Savior."

After Jesus, Mary is the principal figure in the history of salvation. In her culminated all the expectations of the Jewish people who had waited for over a thousand years for a Messiah—the Christ. She was the instrument God used to become man. Through the action of her will, by her perfect faith and ready acceptance of God's will, she became the first to believe in Jesus; she was his first disciple, the perfect Christian, the perfectly redeemed Christian: She heard the word of God and acted upon it, and God became Man. Because she was at all times totally open to the will of God, she is eminently worthy for all Christians to imitate.

Christians honor Mary not just for her preeminent role among men as Mother of God, but for her qualities and traits that are within our reach. Her ready agreement to do the will of God is worthy of imitation by all Christians. Imitating her virtues, however, in no way can be considered as invoking the saints or giving to a creature what rightfully belongs only to God.

Christians cannot forget that is was through Mary, a mere creature of God, that God chose to work their salvation. From the beginning he had willed that his Son, the Second Person of the Trinity, was to become a man like the rest of us, except for sin. God could have accomplished this in any number of ways: he could have chosen to deposit his Son incarnate in a miraculous fashion by some roadside, a man of mystery about whom no one knew anything except that his name was Jesus, a man full-grown and ready to begin his public ministry in much the same fashion as Jesus of the Gospels. Or it might seem that Jesus could have come with a great display of power and majesty as he went about performing fantastic miracles. But such exhibitionism would have been completely out of character with the Jesus we have come to know. Certainly, such a Jesus would never have been able to say of himself, "I am gentle and lowly in heart." Indeed, if this Jesus could ever have been compatible with the mind of God, he would probably now be known primarily as "Jesus, Mighty Wonder-Worker," rather than "Jesus, Lord and Savior."

Instead of a marvelous manifestation of worldly power, God chose to come as a baby. He wanted to be like any other man, to be physically formed from the flesh and blood of a woman and carried in her womb for nine months before being born. And he wanted to be completely dependant on that woman's consent for life itself even though she was his creature. With divine humility, God wanted Jesus to be to her like any child to its mother, with all the prerogatives and demands that go with that relationship—both from mother to child and child to mother.

To understand Mary's role fully, you must again look to the nature of her son. As seen in Chapter IV, Jesus has two natures: he is fully man even though he is God, and these two natures are combined in one person, and that person is God. This does not mean that somehow from all eternity Mary was the mother of the Second Person of the Trinity—that is not only blasphemous but absurd. However, that does not diminish or change the essential truth that Mary, a person created by God in time, became the mother of the *person* of Jesus Christ, and that person, besides taking from her his human nature, was truly God. The early Church formally declared that Mary was the mother of God, not because the Church wanted to bestow a mark of honor or privilege on her, but rather to bring out the true nature of her son Jesus—that the son of Mary is also the Son of God. And later, the Church proclaimed that Jesus is one person with two separate and complete natures—human and divine.

The point is that to understand the nature of Jesus, as well as where Mary fits into the scheme of things, you have to look at them together. Only then does it begin to become clear that Jesus is both fully God and fully man. This is a mystery beyond our full comprehension, of course, something that we can know only through faith. But even though Christians formally believe this, they have a strong tendency to favor, from time to time, either their sense of his divinity or his humanity over the fullness of the other.

As a follower of the Matt Talbot Way, however, you must constantly strive to keep your understanding of Jesus as fully God and fully man, with no diminishment in the nature of either. Without this steady understanding, the Way does not make complete sense. You will not be willing to give up drink for love of Jesus Christ just because he is God—though that ought to be good enough reason. Rather, it will be because he is also man, and *in all his humanity* he suffered and died on the cross for love of you. It is for this Jesus—fully human and fully divine—that you are goaded by love to quit drinking.

If Jesus had been solely God and only wore a thin veneer of humanity like a mask, Mary's "motherhood" would have meant little because she would have contributed little if anything of a human nature to him. She would have been "mother" only to what appeared to be a man. On the other hand, if Jesus had been only a man—a uniquely extraordinary man perhaps, one who could work wonders because of God-given powers, but with no essential difference in nature from the rest of us—who would dream of paying any special attention to his mother? Everyone recognizes Socrates, Gandhi, Beethoven and Lincoln as great men; but who remembers, much less honors or holds up for imitation, their mothers?

Mary became the mother of Jesus, the mother of God, because of her faith and obedience. Only because of her acceptance of God's will was it possible for the rest of his plan for our redemption to proceed. That is not to say that Mary's consent "caused" the salvation event; her consent was simply her opening of herself to receive salvation. In one way, though, it can be said her consent caused salvation: Anyone who receives Christ as Savior then becomes an instrument for Christ to be brought to others. That causation, however, is not the same as Christ's causing salvation.

Mary's essential role in man's salvation cannot be denied, but that does not make her a substitute for the Holy Spirit. She is, however, a perfect model of openness to the working of the Spirit. If the Spirit of Christ is to be formed in us, we can learn from her how to become more open and accommodating to its workings. By listening more intently, we can come to believe more lovingly, and thus be able to respond more creatively. For the follower of the Matt Talbot Way, the uniquely appropriate response is to give up the pleasures of drink for love of Jesus Christ.

Some of the misunderstanding about Catholic reverence for Mary comes about because man tends to exaggerate that which he loves. The extravagance of Catholics' affection for her is often expressed in poetic figures of speech. With flowery language comes overstatements that are not meant to be taken literally—certainly not in a strict theological sense. Once we move beyond the false impressions that such words may engender, all Christians may come to view Mary as the masterpiece of God's creation through the Holy Spirit, thus transcending theological differences.

Particularly since the Second Vatican Council, the Catholic Church has emphasized the imitation of Mary's virtues as the foundation of the proper attitude towards her—an attitude that all Christians can share. Although Catholics and some others like to refer to her as "our" Lady and "our" Blessed Mother, they have no special claim to her: All mankind as brethren of Jesus have an equal right to look upon Mary—the mother of Jesus, the mother of God—as their spiritual mother.

Part Two

A Short Life of Matt Talbot

Tell me, O most sweet lady, Mother of my Lord,
What were your feelings, what your wonder, your joy
When you found your sweetest Son, the boy Jesus.

Jesus at the Age of Twelve
St. Aelred of Rievaulx

Chapter XI

The Early Years

Ireland has long been famous for its saints and missionaries. And everyone is aware of its reputation for drunkards, though few people know that its percentage of abstainers is among the highest in Western countries. In Dublin in 1856, Charles and Elizabeth Talbot never imagined that their newborn son Matt would become like all these types—though not simultaneously to be sure. Matt's parents were to see him progress from an habitual drunkard to a God-driven abstainer; from a weakling who could not stay away from drink to a serene and sober man of extraordinary hidden sanctity. After his death, the story of his spiritual growth would unfold and have a missionary effect on many beyond the shores of Ireland. Lovers of the bottle would be called to become lovers of Jesus Christ.

No Irish layman has ever been canonized a saint; Matt Talbot could well be the first—an uncommonly common man as Saint Matt!

The Talbots had twelve children, of whom Matt was the second. They had little hope for them beyond the expectations of any other poor, working-class family. As the children were growing up, there were few schools and no compulsory education. Many Irish parents preferred to keep their children out of school rather than risk having them lose their Catholic faith in a hostile, secular environment. Much of Matt's early education came while running free in the streets. Eventually, though, he was rounded up with a group of poor boys and sent to a Christian Brothers' school where he received a basic education as well as religious instruction in preparation for receiving the sacraments. Altogether he went to school for only two years; during much of this time he was kept at home because he was needed there. When Matt finished his "schooling" at the age of twelve, he was essentially illiterate.

Soon afterwards he got his first job as a messenger for a firm of wine merchants who were bottlers for Guinness. With easy access to drink in all its glorious varieties, many of the workmen were in the habit of sneaking a little on the side, sometimes to excess. For Matt, the temptation proved too much and he was soon into the stout. When his father caught him coming home tipsy, he gave him a severe thrashing but with no effect.

Matt's father had a position on Dublin's docks, as had his father before him. Thinking he could better keep an eye on his son, he got him a job there as a messenger at the Custom House where bonded liquor was stored. Matt took full advantage of the opportunity; he was now able to complete his apprenticeship in his early vocation as he graduated from stout to whisky. He doggedly pursued his first love and soon was a drunkard.

Because he had got his job through his father's influence, he was a constant embarrassment to him. To spare him further shame, Matt left the Custom House job after a few years. He became a bricklayers' laborer, hauling heavy loads of bricks, cement, planks and other material, up and down ladders at the pleasure of the skilled workers. Because of his short stature and pugnacious nature, he always wanted to prove that he could do as much work as the biggest of his fellow workers. His foreman took advantage of this and usually put him out in front of the other workers to set the pace; he described him as "the best hodman in Dublin." One of his drinking buddies later remarked, "...he'd do more in half an hour than the rest would do in an hour."[1] He could never go easy at anything.

For all his hard work, Matt brought home virtually nothing for his parents' household. Workers were usually paid by a pub owner from funds deposited with him by their employer, it being understood that for this little accommodation, the workers would spend some of their pay there. This was not good enough for Matt, though. Each week he turned over his entire pay in a lump sum to the pub owner with instructions to dole out drinks to him as long as the money lasted. By midweek he would have gone through the money and would begin to drink on his friends' generosity or beg drinks from anyone he could find. Often he came home without his shirt or shoes, having pawned them for more drink.

Saturday being payday, Matt might give his mother Elizabeth a single shilling for the household, all he had left from his week's wages. More often than not, though, he brought her nothing.

All the men in the Talbot household drank except Matt's older brother John. All of them were short, particularly his father Charles, who had that hyper-aggressive demeanor so often seen in small men, as though to make up somehow for short stature. Having a quick temper and a loud voice, he liked to bluster and argue with his sons after a few drinks. Matt and the other boys were much like him, especially in their fondness for drink. Although Matt had the pugnacious nature of his father, he was not usually quarrelsome when drunk.

Elizabeth Talbot naturally had a difficult time holding the family together. Because of the drinking and the consequent poverty—were the Talbots and other poor Dubliners poor because they drank, or did they drink because they were poor?—there was little stability; during the family's first twenty years, they moved eleven times. To make ends meet Elizabeth often worked as a charwoman. It was her persistent prayers and endless rosaries, though, that were both an example to Matt and a means to his later conversion.

Matt had only a rudimentary knowledge of his Catholic faith. He had learned a little about it from his parents, still more from the schooling he got from the Christian Brothers, and especially from the Gospel readings and the sermons at Sunday Mass. As a young man he never missed Sunday Mass, even if drunk the night before. Even if he failed to say his morning prayers, he always signed himself with the cross as he left home for work. Otherwise he was slipshod in the practice of his faith and had stopped going to confession and communion.

From the time that Matt took the job as a bricklayers' laborer, each day settled into a fixed routine divided between work and drink. Off to work by 6:00 A.M., and after a hard day's work, he and his companions would retire to their favorite pub for an evening of gossip and friendly banter, and, of course, serious drinking until closing time. Then, home to sleep it off and begin a new workday at 6:00 A.M. This went on day after day, week after week.

Everything revolved around drink. In her biography, *Matt Talbot and his Times*, Mary Purcell relates an interview she had with Pat Doyle, then in his 90's, one of Matt's early drinking companions. Pat said that Matt "only wanted one thing—the drink, never bothered with parties or dancing or card-playing. But he'd do any mortal thing for drink."[2]

Although Matt would do almost anything for drink, he had a broad streak of honesty—but only up to a point. To buy drinks when their money ran out, Matt and several of his buddies used to play a game with the barmaid. They would distract her attention while one of them edged around to the back of the bar to a barrel of pigs' cheeks in brine, steal one, and then sell it to buy a round of drinks from her. But when Matt's turn came to do the snitching he always seemed to get out of it. His sense of honesty, though, was not so finely tuned that he ever refused the drinks bought with the stolen goods.

Even that limited sense of honesty failed him once; but in the failing, the seeds may have been sown that led him eventually to turn away from drink. A poor, itinerant fiddler had come into the pub, played some tunes, and joined them for a few drinks. While he was at the bar, Matt and one of the boys slipped out with the fiddle, pawned it, and then came back and used the money to buy drinks for themselves and the still unsuspecting fiddler. His thievery was perhaps the only thing he ever did that can be called contemptible. It was to gnaw at his conscience for many years.

Matt was a sociable person, overly generous and fiercely loyal to his friends. While drink was the most important thing in life, he never engaged in solitary boozing. Drinking was always done in the company of his buddies. He was to find out, though, that drink was the only reason for whatever friendship existed among them, and even that friendship didn't carry very far.

It was his sense of solidarity with them that set him up for the most significant day of his life. It was one Saturday, a payday, early in 1884 when he was twenty-eight years old; he hadn't worked for a week but had spent the time drinking. Now he was broke and thirsty as ever; but his friends were due a week's wages so he thought he could count on them. Knowing what he would do if he were in their situation, he went down to the pub to wait for them. He positioned himself so that they couldn't gracefully avoid inviting him to have a few on them. But the most that he got from any of them was "Good day, Matt." He later said that their coldness "cut him to the heart"; in fact, it caused a radical change of heart. Rather than follow them into the pub and directly ask them for a few drinks, he turned and headed home. He decided to give up them and drink for good.

His mother was startled to see him so early. It was the first time in years that he had come home sober on a Saturday. He announced he was going to take "the pledge," to quit drinking "in God's name." This she found difficult to believe—resolutions no doubt had been made before. She told him not to do it unless he really meant it, but with her prayer that "God give you the grace to keep it" ringing in his ears, she sent him on his way. Their prayers were to be answered far beyond what they could have imagined.

That evening Matt told his story to a priest. After going to confession for the first time in years, he took the pledge, though for only three months, fearing that he could not keep it any longer. Sunday morning he went to Mass and Holy Communion. On Monday, to the amazement of his mother, he was up in time for the 5:00 A.M. Mass before going on to work. Thus he began a lifetime of prayer and sobriety.

Matt's motivation for conversion was not due to some personal disaster brought on by drink. Nor was it brought on because of the loss or threatened loss of his job, threats from family members or warnings from doctors—all the usual reasons for people to quit drinking today. Nor, for that matter, was it caused by the hardness of heart of his drinking companions—though he finally saw just how shallow their friendship was. But he did use his hurt pride to help precipitate what had probably been building up for a long time.

One thing that may have moved Matt to face up to the emptiness of his life was the affair with the fiddler. Matt came to bitterly regret what he had done for drink. By nature, he was a kindhearted, generous person. He knew what poverty was about and understood only too well that his love for drink had made him permanently deprive a poor man of his only means of support. His revulsion and horror no doubt grew the more he drank, forcing him to reflect constantly on how low it had brought him. With the callous treatment by his friends on that fateful Saturday, he realized in a flash that their fickleness could be the immediate excuse he needed to turn his back on drink. But neither their indifference, nor for that matter, his meanness towards the fiddler, were the real reasons that he quit drinking; they were simply handy, proximate occasions that he used to help him make up his mind to give it up.

Matt did not realize it but for a long time he had been preparing himself for this moment of grace. He had continued to attend Sunday Mass, even though he had stopped going to the sacraments. He confided to friends later that it was an occasional Hail Mary and pious thoughts about Mary—even when drinking—that became his underlying spiritual support and prepared him for this moment. He knew that he would never be able just to stop drinking unless he found something else to slake his thirst. He had to develop a counter-attraction that in time would overwhelm his love for drink. The only thing possible for him to love more was God—particularly in the person of Jesus Christ. By cultivating friendship and love for Christ, he left no room for drink.

Chapter XII

The New Matt

The first three months of doing without drink were the hardest of Matt's life; his craving for it was as strong as ever. He realized that if he was going to succeed with his pledge, he had to plan carefully his campaign of sobriety. He would never be able to do it without God's help, so he made love of him his primary means of staying sober. He began each day with Mass but since his job as a bricklayers' laborer started at 6:00 A.M., he now had to get up in time for the 5:00 A.M. Mass.

The evenings, however, were a time of potential temptation; he had to steer clear of his old drinking buddies without offending them. Getting along without their companionship would be almost as hard as doing without drink, even though they had failed to prove themselves friends enough to offer him a pint of ale when he needed it most. When they headed for their favorite pub, he went where they would never think of looking for him. The churches of Dublin some distance from home became his favorite haunts. There, until bedtime, he prayed before the Blessed Sacrament, building the foundation of love for Jesus Christ on which his sobriety depended.

Matt also spent every Saturday, after finishing work at noon, and all day Sunday, in church, struggling to pray. For all his willingness, though, he was losing heart. He used to come home at night and confide to his mother that it was no use—when the three months were up, he would go back to drinking. But with her encouragement he held on. At the end of the three months, still fighting on his knees, he began to sense eventual victory. But for the time being, he was only sure enough of himself to renew the pledge for another six months, and then, finally, for life. This gradual feeling of his way was the last time he showed any uncertainty or indecision about the direction of his life.

On one occasion, a few months into his new life, Matt's craving became too much for him. Passing by a pub and feeling money in his pocket, the urge to drink overwhelmed him. After going back and forth several times, he finally went in. Although he waited a long time to be waited on, for some reason no one came to take his order. Finally he found the inner strength to tear himself away and he hurried back to the church he had just left. After that he never carried money with him in the evening in case he should be tempted again, except later when he needed it to give to a charity or someone in need. He stayed out of pubs for good, except to pay back the money he reckoned that he owed on old drinking bills—bills forgotten or written off by the pub owners. For a long time after his conversion, many a Dublin pub owner was surprised when Matt suddenly showed up, handed over an envelope containing money, and then abruptly left.

There was another debt that Matt tried to repay. He spent seven years searching for the fiddler in Dublin's poorhouses and other likely places. He dearly wanted to compensate him for the stolen fiddle, to somehow begin to make up for the awful thing he had done, but he never found him. Finally, assuming he must be dead, he used the money he had set aside to have Masses offered for the repose of his soul.

With his new way of life, Matt eventually found living at home too disruptive. Although he greatly loved his parents and was fond of his brothers and sisters even though the boys drank, the small house became too much for him. He tried to get his brothers to take the pledge, but they scoffed at the idea. So he rented a room not far from home and arranged for his married sister Mary, who lived nearby, to clean it and cook a simple meal for him every day.

Matt never married, though he once received a proposal. He had been working on a building job away from home where several maids and a cook were employed. He caught the eye of the cook because he didn't flirt with the maids or curse and swear like the other men. She introduced herself and got to know him. Finally she suggested marriage, mentioning that she had saved a tidy sum of money they could use to furnish a home. Matt said he would let her know in a week or so, but first he wanted to pray for guidance. When he got back to her, he told her the answer was that he should remain single.

Over the years he gradually added to the routine of spiritual practices that he had begun when he gave up drink. Mass was the high point of each day. He often arrived at church about a half-hour ahead of time and prayed while kneeling on the outside steps, rain or shine, until the doors opened; but if others were around he would wait on the steps of the nearby convent. After Mass, Holy Communion, and the Stations of the Cross, he was home in time for a frugal breakfast before leaving for work. On his way home after work, he stopped in church for a visit to the Blessed Sacrament and to pray the evening Angelus.

After a light supper, he either went to church devotions or to a meeting of one of the religious societies to which he belonged. Or he spent the evening in his room reading spiritual books or in prayer until bedtime.

Every day Matt said all the usual prayers well-known to Catholics, such as the rosary (fifteen decades) and the Angelus (at 6:00 A.M., noon, and 6:00 P.M.), as well as a wide variety of other beads, litanies, and novenas. But prayer for him was far more than reciting formal, set pieces; much of it was the mental and mystical prayer usually associated with monks in contemplative orders. Contemplatives deliberately set themselves physically apart in order to be able to pray with the least distraction from the world. But Matt did not need to actually withdraw from others; he became his own enclosure and learned how to shut out the rest of the world at will. He made the busy streets of Dublin his cloister, his room became his cell, and a secluded spot at work his place of quiet recollection.

Sunday was a full day of prayer for Matt. He was in church from 5:30 A.M. until after Benediction following the last Mass, which was about 1:30 P.M. Except when he went to Holy Communion, he knelt the entire eight hours motionless with hands clasped and eyes closed, absolutely erect, without any support for his arms or hands. Members of the choir remarked that week after week their gaze from the loft was drawn like a magnet to the motionless figure of "Old Reliable" withdrawn in prayer. One man who saw him said, "That man's either a first-class idiot or a first-class saint." A Jesuit priest who once gave him Holy Communion was so struck by the fervor of this unknown man that he remarked to the other priests that there was a saint attending their church. Almost no one knew that Matt had slit the knees of his trousers lengthwise; whenever he knelt, he was able to pull them aside to admit the stone floor, but when he stood up or walked, the holes did not show.

Matt did not adopt his life of prayer and austere practices all at once; rather they were the result of a steady accumulation over the years. His purpose with the austerities was to master his body so that his soul would be more receptive to the workings of the Spirit; thus both body and soul would be liberated from the coils of the world. He began by denying himself drink, but that wasn't nearly enough. He was a heavy pipe smoker, using as much as seven ounces of tobacco a week. One day, a fellow workman asked him for a fill of tobacco. Matt had just bought a new pipe, so he gave him both the pipe and the tobacco. He never smoked again. Until he lost his craving for tobacco, he used to suck on a small white pebble that he carried with him. He confided to a friend that giving up tobacco cost him more than doing without drink. No doubt he exaggerated here, yet there was an element of truth. Drink he had to give up, tobacco he did not; he could easily have continued with his new way of life while still enjoying the simple companionship, even pleasure, of his pipe.

Although we can understand how he got along without alcohol and tobacco, it is difficult to fathom how a manual laborer managed on so little food. Matt never took a full meal after his conversion. During Lent, Advent, the month of June, all Saturdays, and for a week before all major feasts, he went on a "black fast"—two slight meals with no meat, butter, or milk. Fridays were full days of fasts.

But he was always careful to conceal these austerities from outsiders. The only persons who knew about them were family members and a few close friends, and they never talked about him except among themselves. To protect his cover on those rare occasions when he was invited to dinner, Matt always ate what was put before him. Other than when invited out, though, his long procession of colorless meals was broken only on Christmas mornings when he had his sister prepare a small steak as a special treat.

One day when Matt's sister came to tidy his room, she noticed two roughly-planed planks lying against the wall. She asked what they were for, and in an offhand fashion he passed them off saying, "They're for a purpose." Later, when cleaning his room while he was at work, she pulled down the scanty blanket and sheet on his bed and found the "purpose." He was using the planks for a bed and a wooden block as a pillow. In later years, his face became numbed and his hearing impaired from the hard pillow. Matt's planks and pillow, however, pale in comparison with the secret practice that he adopted during the last fourteen years of his life.

During the first years after his conversion, Matt continued to work as a bricklayers' laborer. Because work began at 6:00 A.M., he had to go to the 5:00 A.M. Mass. However, when the hour of the first Mass was changed to 6:15 A.M., he would have had to give up daily Mass if he continued his trade. Rather than do this, he found a job with a lumberyard where work did not begin until 8:00 A.M. He worked here the rest of his life, except towards the end when he was too ill.

In his early days with the lumberyard, Matt had to load and unload ships and trucks on Dublin's docks. He disliked this work because the profanity of the dock workers upset him—he called this his "little failing." Whenever he heard God's name used in vain, he would raise his hat without a word. For awhile it was a good joke to get his hat bobbing as much as possible, though there was no malice in the men's swearing. The joke soon turned sour as they tired of trying to embarrass him. Eventually, he got out of working on the docks altogether. Also, he asked the foreman not to send him to work at the creosote vats where lumber was dipped; he didn't like his clothes to smell of tar when he went to Mass and Holy Communion.

Whenever there was a lull in yard work, Matt would retire to a secluded passage between the lumber stacks to pray. His fellow workers had learned that he did not like to be observed praying, so they would casually announce their approach by coughing, shouting or whistling. Matt didn't think he was breaking any rules; he simply disliked drawing attention to his life of prayer, and his fellow workers respected him for it. Even so, when the bells of the nearby church announced the noon Angelus, he always stopped whatever he was doing for a few moments, took off his hat, and prayed silently. In the evening he usually got away from the yard a few minutes before 6:00 P.M. and ran to the nearby church so that he might be there when the bells rang for the Angelus.

At the entrance to the yard was a gatehouse occupied by one of the workers and his family. One evening after dark, there was a knock at the back door that frightened the lady of the house, as she thought everyone had gone home. It was only Matt, who explained that he had been "saying a few prayers" and did not notice the dark coming on; as the yard gate was locked, would she let him out through the house.

After a few years at the lumberyard, Matt was promoted to storeman, a less physically-demanding job. In this job he had to check the materials entering and leaving the yard as well as to help load and unload the trucks. He had the use of a shack between the lumber stacks as his "office." Between the coming and going of trucks, or when the work was slow and he had nothing to do, he would quietly withdraw to his office to pray without being observed.

Matt was a conscientious worker. He was never late for work or wasted time; this would have outraged his sense of honesty—like stealing from his employer. He was determined to give the fullest possible return for his wages. For example, when a cargo of timber had to be unloaded quickly for the ship to catch the outgoing tide, the workmen were offered a bonus if they finished the job in time. This required several hours of exhausting work; but when the crew earned its bonus, Matt would not call at the office to pick up his share. He did not think he was entitled to anything extra since he was often idle while waiting for trucks. The foreman insisted that he accept the bonus on this and other occasions. But he would never claim the money, and the foreman always had to bring it to him; he would then accept it only as a gift. Anyway, he simply gave the extra money to charity.

Matt was not willing to accept his limited reading skill; he spent years of labored effort to master the mechanics of reading. Because he could go only at a snail's pace at first, what he read made a deep impression. He usually spent several hours a day reading, and because he considered it a form of prayer, he always read on his knees. Eventually he was reading a remarkable range of books—from the Bible to profound works on theology, to obscure treatises on mysticism.

His library contained nearly one hundred books, many of them comprising several volumes, such as St. Augustine's *Confessions* in ten volumes. He owned several copies of the whole Bible and the New Testament. St. Matthew's Gospel appears to have been his favorite account of the Passion, though he apparently had read each evangelist's account a great many times—these pages were worn almost to shreds.

Matt constantly borrowed books from acquaintances. He read such spiritual classics as St. Francis de Sales' *Introduction to the Devout Life*, Thomas à Kempis' *The Imitation of Christ*, and Butler's *Lives of the Saints*. And there were countless individual lives of saints such as Catherine of Siena, Teresa of Avila, and Thomas More. But his reading was not limited to spiritual books; he read many works with titles such as *History of the Roman Empire*, *History of Peter the Great of Russia*, *Between Capitalism and Socialism*, and *A Living Wage and a Family Wage*.

One day a fellow-worker, seeing that Matt was reading Cardinal Newman's *Apologia Pro Vita Sua*—Matt eventually read all his works—mentioned that he had tried it but gave it up as being over his head. Matt said that before he read a book, he always prayed to God for light to understand the main points. He thought he always managed to understand most of what he read. When he came across a passage he found obscure, he often copied it down on a scrap of paper, and after his next confession, would pass it to the surprised priest and ask for help in understanding it.

Matt took little interest in politics. He all but ignored the great events of the day—the World War, the Rising of 1916, the Anglo-Irish war of 1919-1921 and the later "troubles"—as being matters beyond his control. He was so completely taken up with the things of God, little room was left for anything else. For all of his detachment, though, he was keenly sensitive to the rights of workers to a just wage. He was not concerned for himself; he didn't need more money—anything extra he gave away. But he saw that his fellow unskilled workers were being paid little more than starvation wages, making it almost impossible for the married ones to survive. Once when he spoke out about the low pay of married workers, he was spitefully passed over when the next raises were handed out.

His participation in Dublin's "Big Strike" in 1913 was the closest he ever got to politics. Dublin's dock strike in 1900 was unsuccessful, and the Big Strike was the inevitable result. This time the workers were far better organized. Matt belonged to the union but didn't attend its meetings, preferring to leave its decisions to others. Eventually the strike involved the lumberyard, and Matt went out with the rest of the men. He was an enthusiastic supporter of the workers and their right to strike, but he refused to picket as he did not believe that it was right to prevent others from working; he thought that was an even greater injustice than paying inadequate wages.

Strike pay was supposed to go only to those who went on the picket line. Even though Matt had not, the union unanimously voted him a full share. The union recognized that his extraordinary Christian attitude set him apart from the others, and that he shouldn't be judged by the same standards. He would never pick up the money, though, and someone always had to bring it to him. Because his financial needs were minimal, the extra money permitted him to help some of the married workers through "loans."

In looking over Matt Talbot's life, what is striking is that there was nothing unusual, as least not as the world judges these things—only an unrelenting grayness. His life had no features except religious ones. And even these, almost without exception, were hidden and completely lacking in highlights. His life of prayer and mortifications involved a steady, persistent practice throughout his life of what he set for himself. He often said, "It is constancy God wants." His life of prayer and penance was not something that an old man might adopt who finally "got religion" when he didn't have anything better to do except wait around to die. Matt was a vigorous young man of twenty-eight when he began to take on the remarkable burdens that grew over the years. He found time for his uncommon catalogue of prayers and other religious practices only after putting in ten hours or so of manual work each day.

The only notable events during his later years were the deaths of his parents. His father died in 1899, which resulted in his mother coming to live with him in his rented room. In the evening, if he did not attend a meeting of some church society or other devotions, he talked with her about religious matters or read to her. It was a cheerful and happy time, as he was devoted to her. These final twelve years were the pinnacle of her own life of prayer, a marvelous contrast to those sixteen dark years when her St. Monica-like prayers for her wayward son seemed to go unanswered.

Chapter XIII

The Inner Man

"If I done the things that he done, they would put me in the madhouse"—so remarked a neighbor of Matt after he died.[1] Far from belonging in an insane asylum, Matt was a practical, down-to-earth sort of person, untroubled by events that swirled about him. He was not crazy, though you might expect that his fasts and mortifications would have at least reduced him to a gloomy, dispirited man, carrying around some unseen weight, out of sorts with the rest of the world. Although he kept much to himself, he was no eccentric recluse. An agreeable, compassionate man, he was easily approached, always ready to help others any way he could. Habitually cheerful and in good humor, he often seemed ready to break into a smile when not actually smiling.

There was nothing striking or impressive about his appearance. He was of short but wiry build, and as described by one of his fellows, "strong as a little horse." It is difficult to understand how anyone ate as little as he did without becoming a pasty, worn-out figure, unable to do hard work. On the contrary, he had an immense store of energy. Always in a hurry, he often seemed to run rather than walk. His close friends knew that he usually prayed the rosary privately as he hurried about.

Although his clothes were always of poor quality he was unusually clean and tidy. One of his economies came from never buying clothes because of hand-me-downs and gifts. Invariably they didn't fit because of his short stature. On one occasion some of the ladies of his parish had become tired of seeing him always poorly dressed and wanted to buy him some new clothes. They enlisted the help of a parish priest in the delicate task of speaking to him about it. Matt sidestepped them, though, by confiding to the priest that he had promised God he would never wear good clothes.

His basic honesty was revealed by his blunt speech. He hated pretense of any kind, and when he thought he was right, he spoke openly to everyone, no matter what their position. As he had inherited his father's pugnacity, he was by nature a bit hot-tempered; still, he managed to keep this under control and was ordinarily quite mild-mannered. If things went wrong, though, he could become aroused; then he would usually walk away in silence and calm down. At times, though, he would lose his temper for a few moments; but if he said something hurtful to anyone, he would return later and offer a sincere apology.

Matt was generous by nature. He had no personal use for money except to provide for bare essentials. If he loved God, he had to love his neighbor, too—money was handy here. Several times he gave a fellow worker the price of a pair of boots. In making gifts he had a marvelous winning manner—running off before he could be thanked. Usually his generosity was cast in the form of "loans." He insisted on repayment, otherwise the easy money might tempt some to spend it in a pub. However, many of these loans were disguised gifts and were never repaid.

He "lent" a considerable amount of money to fellow workers

who had families. A loan was never refused to anyone as long as there was a real need. But any fellow who came to him on a Monday morning for a loan after having spent his wages in a pub over the weekend got short shrift. But he was not narrow-minded about drink; on occasion he gave a man the price of a drink, saying that "a pint of porter never did anyone any harm."

Matt's neighbors were often touched by his generosity. One evening a lady who lived in the same tenement knocked on his door. Apparently she had interrupted him while he was praying, for he was quite grumpy. She told him that she was behind in her rent and would be evicted if what amounted to approximately $7.50 in American currency was not paid by the next day. He went back into his room and returned with the money, asking her to pay him back when she could, but to leave him alone for now. The money was never repaid.

Matt's gifts to charity were astonishing. By following an austere diet and never buying new clothes, his personal financial needs were minimal. In this way he was able to give away most of his income. Throughout most of his life, his wages were the equivalent of about $5 a week.[2] He spent about $1.20 for rent and the little food he allowed himself, with the rest going to charity. After the Big Strike in 1913, his wages tripled to $15; he now needed about $2 for himself (union dues and burial insurance causing the increase in his personal expenses). The extra income simply meant that he could give away that much more to those in need.

Matt was well known as a soft touch by fund raisers; he regularly sent money to the Poor Clares, an orphanage in New York, and many local charities. The Jesuit brother who unlocked the church door for the first Mass often had money thrust into his hand with the charge that it be used for the poor. Once he gave money to a priest while he was in the confessional, asking that it be used for charity. When the priest finally saw that it was a five pound note, he began to ask his name, but Matt was already gone.

On one occasion, a priest had been allowed to put up a notice at the lumberyard that on a particular payday he would be taking up a collection for a poor parish in a distant part of Ireland. When the day arrived the men were generous, each giving a shilling or two. When the priest had finished taking up the collection, the foreman told him that he had overlooked a man at the end of the yard and suggested that he go and talk to him. When the priest returned, he said in astonishment that he never met anyone so generous—the man had given him all the money he had on him. Matt had just been paid his week's wages, which in those days amounted to about $15.

Matt's imagination had been caught up by the Maynooth Mission to China maintained by the Columban Fathers. His generosity and zeal reached new heights as every month he sent them what for him were large sums of money. He told his foreman that he gave them $150 a year, not as an idle boast but in an effort to get the foreman to increase his own donations to the mission.

Another kind of charity also moved Matt. Many people had heard that his prayers were extraordinarily effective, and eagerly sought his assistance. He was always willing to try to help, with the understanding that regardless of the outcome, the will of God must be accepted without reservation. Monsignor Hickey, President of Holy Cross College, and for years Matt's confessor and spiritual advisor, used to tell others that when he wanted a special favor, he always had a poor man named Matt Talbot pray for it. He said his prayers were always answered.

Until near the end of his life, Matt was always in good health, which is quite surprising, considering the many years of hard work with so little nourishment. In 1923, when he was sixty-seven years old, his health began to fail; heart trouble was diagnosed. Twice he was sent to the hospital that year and twice he received the last rites. When he left the hospital the second time he was unable to work. For the next year and a half he lived in dire poverty, with a weekly insurance benefit of $1.88 his only income. Out of this paltry amount he had to pay his rent and buy his food and other necessities. There was nothing left over for anything else—or so it would seem.

His friends had pressed upon him a few small gifts of money from which he was able to set aside a rainy-day fund of $7.50. But from his weekly insurance benefit, there was nothing left over for his dear charities. This did not pass unnoticed. The priest who directed the fund-raising for the Maynooth Mission missed Matt's regular donations. In December of 1924 he sent him a Christmas greeting and inquired about his health. In response, Matt sent the only letter he was known to have written:

> Matt Talbot have done no work for past 18 months. I have been sick and given over by Priest and Doctor. I don't think I will work any more. There one pound from me and ten shillings from my sister.

Matt sent his entire savings, about $7.50, with $2.50 of it given in the name of his sister in appreciation for her taking care of him during his illness. His "widow's mite" was four times his weekly insurance benefit. Everything he had was now gone. It would seem that he had received in abundance what he asked for in one of his favorite prayers: "O Blessed Mother, obtain from Jesus a share of his folly."

During the final weeks and months of illness and physical decline, Matt kept up his usual routine, except when it was impossible. Some concessions had to be made: He could no longer spend entire Sunday mornings in church as in the old days; now he had to come home after the first Mass for a small breakfast and a rest before completing his morning in church. His sister checked up on him every morning and often found him lying on his plank bed, exhausted from walking home from Mass. He could not speak until he had rested a bit and regained his strength. Thinking that Matt might die suddenly, on one occasion she suggested that she should return later in the day and stay with him. He answered simply, "What good could you do? If I die here I shall have Jesus and Mary with me."

In April 1925, Matt began to feel better and went back to work at the lumber yard. He looked ill and worn out, but he still managed to put in a full day doing light work. The first Saturday in June he told his foreman that he felt as well as ever. The next day, Trinity Sunday and June 7, he went to an early Mass and returned for breakfast and a rest as was his habit. Later that morning, he left to attend a second Mass, a walk of about twenty minutes. He had almost reached the church when he collapsed and died.

Matt had no identification in his pockets—only a rosary and a prayer book. His body was brought to the morgue to await the arrival of a claimant. When the threadbare clothes were being cut from his body, one of the attendant's scissors struck something hard—it was chains. They didn't know what to make of it except as one of them said, "He's either a madman or a saint." They found a heavy chain around the waist, two lighter ones around an arm and a leg, and a cord twisted around the other arm. The heavier chains had links similar in weight to those of an automobile snow chain. It is uncertain how long Matt had worn them or if he followed the practice continuously.

Ordinarily, a plank bed, a wooden pillow, and little food would be sufficient to satisfy the needs of the most penitential-minded person. But this was not enough for Matt. It appears that about 1912 he had begun to wear chains occasionally after reading Blessed Louis Marie Grignon de Monfort's book, *True Devotion to the Blessed Virgin Mary*. (Louis was canonized in 1947 and is now known as St. Louis de Montfort.) Louis advised the aspirant after a deeper spiritual life to wear a "little chain" as a *symbol* of having "voluntarily surrendered himself to the glorious slavery of Jesus Christ," much as one might wear a necklace with a medal or a spouse might put a ring on a finger as an outward sign of total commitment in marriage. In his usual fashion of not going easy at anything, and contrary to the teaching of Louis, Matt chose to interpret this literally and in a penitential way. He decided that the chains he would use should directly impress upon his body a sign of the passion of Christ, as well as to remind him that he had voluntarily bound himself over as a slave.[3]

Too much should not be made of Matt's chains, though. They were just one of the means he used to bring his body under his complete control. More important, they were a living symbol of his holy bondage to Christ. In the end, though, they became the means that brought his entire life before the world. God, it would seem, unmasked him in his own good time. If Matt had not been wearing chains when he died, it is unlikely that we would know anything about him today.

The suddenness of Matt Talbot's death exposed him as "The Man in Chains" and caught the imagination of Dublin and all Ireland. People wanted to know more about this poor man, this common workman who had been driven to put on irons. But Matt was never one to wear his life of prayer and penance on his sleeve, and his family always kept quiet about him. However, he did reveal a little about his spiritual life to a few people whom he thought likely to adopt a particular practice—"If I can do it, so can you." To anyone who would listen and show a lively interest, he loved to talk about spiritual matters. Most of his fellow workers and neighbors, however, had no idea of his hidden life. Still, many of them were able to give bits and pieces of information about him, which when put together like little pieces of shiny, colored glass, formed a mosaic likeness of him.

Raphael O'Callaghan, a wine merchant who was Matt's confidant and friend of twenty-five years, had a fairly good knowledge of his spiritual life. It was he, a taller man than Matt, who gave him the clothes that fit so poorly. After Matt died, he spoke to Sir Joseph Glynn, a friend and a lawyer, and suggested that he write a short sketch about the poor man he had known. Glynn wrote a pamphlet that was published a few months later. It was highly successful: within a few months, 120,000 copies were sold, and within a year, was translated into twelve languages.

Glynn was pressed to do a longer work, one that would give more details of Matt's daily life, especially the part that was almost completely hidden from the world. His lawyer's skills served him well; he interviewed many of the people who had known Matt and sifted through a mass of information. The results of this second effort, *Life of Matt Talbot*, was published in 1928 and was also very successful.

By 1931 Matt Talbot's reputation for saintliness was widespread, generated in large part by Glynn's two works. This helped set in motion an inquiry by the Catholic Church to determine whether Matt's apparent sanctity justified him to be considered for sainthood. Many of the people who had known him testified under oath and the results were submitted to Rome, which later issued a formal decree authorizing his "cause." A second inquiry was held in 1949, when many of the same witnesses again testified. As a result of this continuing process, in 1975 the Church bestowed on him the title of "Venerable," meaning that he was judged fit to be recommended to all as a model or hero whose virtues were worthy of imitation.

Chapter XIV

Spiritual Motivation

Before his conversion, all Matt wanted was to drink. Later in life, he still wanted only one thing, but then it was God. Looking back over his life for the underlying reason for his change, what stands out was his need for friends. He was the sort of person who had to have friends upon whom he could lavish his natural affection and generosity. Only after his drinking companions proved themselves false was he able to find his true Friend, Jesus Christ. His life became filled with this new Friend. He was able to slake one thirst only by developing another—the "I thirst" of Jesus on the cross became his own thirst for the love of Christ. He became ecstatic—intoxicated, if you will—with love for him.

But first Matt had to get to know Jesus. In the early days of his conversion, he got away from his old friends during the dangerous evening hours by hiding out in the churches of Dublin. Soon the churches became his second home. Here he spent hour after hour with his new Friend, begging for the gift of prayer itself and for the strength to persevere in his new life. He prayed before the Blessed Sacrament with that devotion which, as Frank Sheed has noted, is "not adoration, though adoration is, of course, there, but sheer companionability."[1] He never seemed to get enough of the company of Christ.

After those early months, Matt continued to make several visits each day to Christ in the Blessed Sacrament. These were like anyone's visit to his warmest and closest neighborhood friend. Once a lady grumbled to him how lonely she had become since her favorite brother left for America. "Lonely!" exclaimed Matt, "How can anyone be lonely? With our Lord always in his tabernacle where anyone can visit him? That's nonsense!"

But Matt wanted more than mere friendship; he wanted to grow in likeness to Jesus. In the Gospels, the Father proclaimed that Jesus was his Son "with whom I am well pleased" (Matthew 3:17; 17:5). Matt believed that if the Father was to be pleased with him, it would be because he bore a resemblance to Jesus, and that the Father saw in him, to a certain degree at least, his Son. Matt's first step in working this transformation (though at all times it was really the Holy Spirit responding to him) was to focus on Jesus—particularly in his humanity. Matt developed a strong admiration for him as a person, learning as much as possible about what sort of person he was. Here, spiritual reading was indispensable. But this was only one of the steps: he coupled his growing admiration for Jesus with prayer and the sacraments.

His reception of Holy Communion at daily Mass was a most intimate encounter. Jesus Christ was more truly present to him after receiving Communion than was an acquaintance with whom he might be speaking later. Although the Real Presence of Christ is the same for all communicants, most perceive it in only a halfhearted fashion; few actually believe it in the sense that their whole being rejoices in it and is possessed by it. But for Matt, it was the ultimate reality of each day. Sean O'Kelly, who became President of Ireland, was an altar boy at Matt's church. After Matt's death, O'Kelly testified that "he seemed to be as humble a type of man as one could meet. He seemed completely lost to what happened around him when he was praying. I would say that he was the nearest I could imagine to one in ecstasy... his manner in the church before Holy Communion was most reverent."[2]

The frequency of Matt's reception of Communion was revolutionary. In the 1880's and 1890's, it was customary for "good" laymen to receive Communion only twice a year, at Christmas and Easter. From the time of his conversion in 1884, however, Matt received Communion daily. He anticipated by some twenty years Pope Pius X's decree in 1905 recommending daily Communion.

The Stations of the Cross was a favorite devotion. He made the way with Christ each day to express his solidarity with him. He confided to a friend that he would have preferred to move from station to station entirely on his knees but felt that would draw too much attention to himself.

As a result of these daily encounters with Christ, Matt was becoming more Christlike. To be more receptive to the Spirit of Christ, he brought his body and its appetites into complete subjugation to his will. Where before he had been a slave to his body, now his body would be his slave. He reasoned that if he could only reduce his need for food, sleep, and comfort to an absolute minimum, he would be more readily receptive, more quickly responsive, to the prompting of the Holy Spirit.

Like anyone who comes to admire and love someone, there is a strong tendency to want to be like that person. It was only natural that Matt should want to imitate Jesus—in his principles, the way he thought, and the way he lived. With Matt's directness and generosity of action, his plank bed and chains were almost an inevitable step in that direction—for him, if for no one else. In any event, they were never meant to be an end in themselves—only the means of bringing about a closer union with Jesus. They were his way of expressing his consuming admiration and compassion for the suffering and crucified Christ.

In his biography of Matt Talbot, Eddie Doherty best describes Matt's longing to become one with Christ: "Who that makes his bed on a hard plank can fail to imagine how Christ felt, lying on the cross, with the nails holding fast His hands and His feet, the ropes binding His arms to the wood, and the thorns digging deeper into His head with every movement of His body? Who that uses a block of wood for a pillow can help thinking of the agony of the crown of thorns? …A man waking on a cross of his own devising must regard it as only a minor thing to remain, absorbed in contemplation, for a few hours, on his knees."[3]

The bond which formed between Matt and Jesus Christ was the cornerstone of his spiritual life. In no way, however, did this interfere with his love for Mary, his spiritual mother. Nor did his devotion to her detract in the least from the praise and adoration due only to God. These were two entirely different relationships. Like any son, he had a warm, personal love for her. In this he believed he was simply adopting Jesus' own attitude of love and respect for his mother. If Jesus Christ—the Son of God—found it fitting to submit so completely to her during the first thirty years of his life (and give glory to his Father by doing so), certainly Matt could only please his Father by loving and respecting her as his spiritual mother, too.

Matt looked upon Mary as the perfect model to imitate if he was to grow in love for Jesus. He knew she wanted to share with him the secret of her joy, which was Jesus himself. He never let himself forget that Jesus' first miracle of grace was performed at the sound of her voice, when Elizabeth received the gift of prophecy and John the Baptist was sanctified in his mother's womb. Matt knew, of course, that it was not Mary who performed these miracles of grace; rather, it was the Holy Spirit through the Child whom she was carrying. Still, it was her voice that seemed to move God to act. He believed that Jesus was still attentive to her, and that the continuing mother-son relationship in no way detracted from his divinity. For his part, Matt was attentive to Mary's words, too: he always tried to follow the instructions she had given to the servants at Cana—"Do whatever he tells you" (John 2:5). In speaking about his old life of drinking, he often said, "Where would I be only for God and his Blessed Mother?" and "No one knows the good mother she has been to me."

To begin to understand the affection that the Irish and people like Matt Talbot have for Mary, an old story recounted by G.K. Chesterton lays bare their heart. He related how he had heard in Donegal of someone coming upon a beautiful peasant woman wandering in the rocky wastes and carrying a child. Upon being asked her name, the woman answered simply: "I am the Mother of God, and this is Himself, and He is the boy you will all be wanting at the last."[4] For all their affection and devotion for Mary, they save their adoration for Himself—He is the One they will all be wanting at the last.

Chapter XV

MATT'S HEROES

As happens with friendships, the friends of Jesus became Matt's friends. As an avid reader of the lives of the saints, Matt developed an easy familiarity with them as one does with close friends and family members. He believed that time spent in social conversation with someone that could not be turned to talking about the lives of the saints and spiritual matters was wasted. Once he got to know someone, he loved to chat about these things as though they were family matters.

After Mass he often took time to pet a beautiful collie that used to lie in the vestibule of the church, and so he got to know the lady who owned it. One afternoon she called on him at his room to give him a few eggs, for he recently had been in the hospital. Matt soon turned the conversation to spiritual matters. He spoke with a charming ease and familiarity about the Gospels, his favorite saints and Mary. His guest later told how she was "quite entranced with his conversation, which was very beautiful." She thought she had been with him for only half an hour but it turned out to be three hours.[1]

Matt was especially fond of St. Catherine of Siena and St. Teresa of Avila. But three other saints are singled out here as having had a pronounced influence on him: St. Francis of Assisi, St. Louis de Montfort (he was not canonized until 1947 and until then was better known as Blessed Louis Marie Grignion de Montfort) and St. Thérèse of Lisieux (canonized only a few weeks before Matt died). The highlights of their lives, particularly the spiritual aspects, are related here because anyone who wants to follow the Matt Talbot way would do well to know a little about Matt's heroes.

St. Francis of Assisi

St. Francis is often captured in picture and stone as a lover of birds and animals. Indeed, the universal reverence in which he is held is explained in part because he is seen as having been kind to animals. The underlying basis for this imagery is not so much that he was fond of animals—though he was—but rather that he saw in all creation a reflection of God's love. Because of this, he was devoted to all created things, animate and inanimate. On hearing a bird sing, he often raised his mind to God, joyfully praising and thanking him for this new evidence of his presence and love. And since all men are not only creatures of God, but cast in the image of Jesus, all of them demanded his respect and love, no matter how low their condition. Water reminded him that Christ used it in his first miracle and that it had flowed from his side when he was pierced by the lance. Bread and wine brought to mind that Christ had changed these into his body and blood. In short, he took delight in all of God's works and saw everything leading him to Christ.

As a young man, Francis was known for his merrymaking and reckless extravagance. His love for the good life made him the natural leader of Assisi's young men. As the son of a wealthy cloth merchant, he had enough money to satisfy his passing whims. Decked out in the fanciest clothes, he presided at lavish parties with his friends, after which they would wander through the streets at midnight, singing songs of courtly love. For all his carousing, though, he did not seem to have had any serious moral lapses. Nor was he so recklessly extravagant with himself and his fun-loving fellows that he had nothing left for the poor—his self-indulgence was exceeded only by his generosity towards beggars and others in need.

One day while praying in St. Damian's, a country church badly in need of repair, he heard a voice from a crucifix: "Go, Francis, and repair my house, for as you see, it is in ruins." Later, after a dramatic confrontation with his father, he made a complete break, not only with his family and friends, but also with the prevailing spirit of love of money and possessions.

He began to evangelize the world in the spirit of poverty as he went about proclaiming the Gospel in simple terms that anyone could understand. Most important was his example—he practiced what he preached, taking for himself the poorest and simplest way of life, devoid of all possessions, begging as he went, never forgetting that his Master had had no place to lay his head. He would serve the poor, but he would be poorer than any of those he served.

Although poverty was the fundamental principle of his way of life, it was not the sordid, miserable condition from which everyone naturally shrinks. It was a happy state because he had stripped himself of those things of the world that have always come between man and God. Poverty was never an end in itself, only a means to facilitate receiving the spirit of Christ. True wealth was to be had, not by coveting and clinging to possessions, but by stripping oneself of things in order to be better able to pursue that which had lasting value.

At the outset Francis had no intention of forming a religious order, but his brotherhood (out of humility he called it the Friars Minor or Little Brothers) grew with such phenomenal speed that within a few years thousands of Friars swept through Europe proclaiming the Gospel in their simple fashion. People of all strata of society—young and old, rich and poor, single and married—wanted to follow him, but this obviously was not possible. So he formed a Third Order Secular to satisfy these. (The Second Order was the "Poor Clares" founded by St. Clare under the guidance of Francis.) In this way even those who were married and raising children could live in conformity to Franciscan ideals. Dante, Giotto, King St. Louis of France and Queen St. Elizabeth of Hungary became members, as well as thousands of the poor and unknown.

The rule of the Third Order was disarmingly simple: apply the precepts of the Gospel to everyday life. In a spirit of poverty, men and women of every class were able to live a truly Christian life even when pursuing their vocation in a busy world. Material poverty is no guarantee of sanctity, of course: the most abject pauper can be consumed by avarice, envy and greed, but a spirit of poverty can be cultivated even by the wealthy. Tertiaries, as members of the Third Order became known, were imbued with the spirit of otherworldliness which characterized Francis, but they achieved this without raising barriers between themselves and the rest of the world. They viewed the world as a place that should be transformed by the spirit of Christ. Rather than renounce the world and all its delights and pleasures, they sanctified it by following both the Golden Rule and a rule of golden moderation in all things.

To Francis, Jesus Christ was not only the Son of God, but the son of Mary. During the first few centuries of the Church, it had been primarily concerned with establishing that Jesus Christ was the incarnate Son of God. As a result, in the early Middle Ages, theologians continued to stress his divinity (though without in any way denying his humanity), and this was reflected in the way Christians perceived him. But Francis understood that people could better learn to love Christ if they focused more on his humanity—that the Son of God came into the world as a baby, lived as a poor man, and suffered and died on the cross for love of all of them. As a way to bring out the humanity of Christ, Francis and his followers popularized the devotions of the Christmas creche, the Angelus, the Stations of the Cross, and meditations on Christ's passion, his Sacred Heart and the Holy Eucharist.

Of all devotions which emphasized Christ's humanity, it was those that emphasized the suffering Christ, the crucified Christ, to which Francis was particularly drawn. Whatever might remind him of this could set him to meditating on him: a crucifix obviously had this power, but even the sight of two crossed timbers in the distance might be enough for his mind's eye to see Christ on the cross. Francis's influence was so far-reaching that the thirteenth century, which began in an atmosphere of indifference to Christ, is now renowned for the pervasive love of Christ expressed by Christians at all levels of society.

St. Francis of Assisi has become the most popular saint, not only with Catholics. He is revered by many Protestants, as well as people who are not even Christians. In fact, there is a Protestant Third Order of St. Francis.

It was only natural that Matt Talbot should be drawn to St. Francis. Matt was known to all as a man who had little use for money, at least as far as his own needs were concerned: "Everyone loves Matt; he don't care for money." Although he had already committed himself to a life of sanctity, in 1890 he became a member of the Third Order, known today as the Franciscan Secular Order. During his lifetime there were over three million members throughout the world. As a Tertiary, he said a few special prayers each day, observed a few days of fast and abstinence, and attended monthly meetings (during his first twenty years he missed only two). The other obligations of the rule, such as daily Mass if possible, unpretentiousness and simplicity in dress, temperance in food and drink, and the avoidance of dangerous pleasures, were already a part of his way of life. But Matt took pains to conceal his life of prayer and penance even from his fellow Tertiaries.

An important part of the Tertiary's rule is the active practice of charity towards all. It is here that Matt became a perfect model of what a Tertiary can be. His generosity towards his fellow workers and neighbors seemed to know no bounds. When it came to making financial gifts to further the mission of the Church—such as the Maynooth Mission to China—Matt tried to empty himself in following the example of Jesus and Francis. Although his income was modest, being single he could have lived quite comfortably. He chose instead to deny himself at every turn and live a life of material poverty, as he went about living serenely in the world, even while he was not of the world.

St. Louis de Montfort

Father Louis de Montfort, an itinerant preacher in western France during the early eighteenth century, gave some two hundred retreats and missions during his sixteen short years as a priest. As he went around preaching his missions, which emphasized love for the crucified Christ, he arranged whenever possible to have a large cross or crucifix erected. In some cases he set up crosses and statues to represent the entire Crucifixion scene. Some of these Crucifixion scenes still stand. His purpose was to give the people a continuing reminder that Christ died for each of them.

He also preached devotion to Mary as the mother of Jesus, the mother of God. Wherever he preached his missions, he established what he called the Perfect Devotion to the Blessed Virgin, not just for the "devout" few among them but even for the most abject of sinners. It required the daily praying of the rosary even after the mission ended. Over a hundred and fifty years later, the bishops of western France were still marveling at the lasting impression that his love of the Cross and his devotion to Mary had on the faith of the people of their dioceses.

Louis de Montfort pursued his missionary work at a time when Jansenism was flourishing within the Catholic Church. The Jansenists had a pessimistic view of the world and of human nature, maintaining that everything in it was evil. They taught that those who are saved were predestined by God for salvation, that grace was irresistible to these elect, and that man did not have freedom of will. They didn't believe that Jesus died for all men; rather, they looked upon him as a severe, distant redeemer, difficult if not impossible to approach except for the elect. The Jansenists had lost sight of the true nature of Jesus—that in his single person resided a fully developed human nature along with his divine nature. They greatly emphasized his divinity over his humanity, resulting in a Christ as aloof as God had been perceived through the Scriptures before the Incarnation. God was seen not as a Father to be loved, but as an avenging judge to be feared.

Needless to say, the Jansenists were opposed to the devotional practices of Louis de Montfort. They hated his direct approach to the crucified Christ and his deep devotion to Mary. Holy Communion was meant only for a select few; devotion to Mary was akin to idolatry.

Although he was primarily a preacher, it is through his writings that he continues to exert a remarkable influence. The manuscript of what was to become his most important work was not discovered until 1842, over a century after his death. In this book, *True Devotion to the Blessed Virgin Mary*, he outlined the same devotion to Mary as he had instructed the people during his missions. Since it was first published it has had an extraordinary effect on countless Catholics, including Matt Talbot. Louis de Montfort was probably Matt's favorite spiritual writer after the Evangelists. In Matt's day he had not yet been canonized and was known as Blessed Louis Marie Grignion de Montfort.

In his book Louis de Montfort calls for Christians to imitate Mary's *fiat*—"Be it done to me as you say; I am the maid servant of the Lord." Like Mary, they should accept the Holy Spirit and allow the likeness of Jesus Christ to be formed within them. They too could become servants or slaves of the Lord in the same fashion as St. Paul repeatedly referred to himself as Christ's "slave." As a *symbol* of this holy bondage, Father Louis recommended the wearing of a medal on a necklace or little chain. Although his words were clear enough, Matt in his usual fashion of doing everything to excess, chose to understand them as a call not only for a chain that would be a sign of his bondage to Christ, but a chain heavy and uncomfortable enough to remind him constantly of Christ's sufferings.

True Devotion continues to draw Catholics more closely to Jesus Christ. Pope John Paul II, for example, said that when he read it, it was "a decisive turning-point in my life." He goes on: "My devotion to the Mother of Christ in my childhood and adolescence yielded to a new attitude.... Whereas originally I held back for fear that devotion to Mary should mask Christ instead of giving him precedence, I realized... that the situation was really quite different. Our inner relation to the Mother of God derives from our connection with the mystery of Christ. There is, therefore, no question of the one preventing us from seeing the other.... 'True devotion' to the Virgin Mary is revealed more and more to the very person who advances into the mystery of Christ, the Word incarnate, and into the trinitarian mystery of salvation which centers round this mystery. One can even say that just as Christ on Calvary indicated his mother to the disciple John, so he points her out to anyone who strives to know and love him."[2]

The motto of John Paul II, "Totus Tuus" (I am totally yours), is a summation of *True Devotion*.

St. Thérèse of Lisieux

The influence of St. Thérèse on Matt Talbot was probably not as direct as that of Francis of Assisi or Louis de Montfort. When Matt first heard of her, he was already well set in his spiritual ways. Still, her spiritual teaching affirmed and reinforced what he had otherwise learned from the Scriptures and the lives of the saints.

Thérèse entered the Carmelite convent at Lisieux at the age of fifteen. Before she was allowed in at such a young age, she had to besiege various authorities, including the Pope, for permission. As a cloistered nun, she did nothing but pray, obey, do simple household chores and act as novice mistress. But everything she did, she did very well, and she did it all for love of God—"That shall be my life, to scatter flowers—to miss no single opportunity of making some small sacrifice, here by a smiling look, there by a kindly word, always doing the tiniest things right, and doing it for love."[3]

In this way she was able to pack a whole lifetime of love into a short life. She died in agony from tuberculosis in 1897 at the age of twenty-four. Soon after her death her autobiography was published from several manuscripts she had written at the direction of her superiors. The book began to sweep the world, and she was acclaimed by the public as a saint—"the Little Flower"—even before the Church gave its approval. The Church beatified her in 1923 and canonized her in 1925, an extraordinarily short time for such things. She is often referred to as the greatest saint of modern times and in 1997 was declared a Doctor of the Church by Pope John Paul II.

Thérèse was especially appealing to the ordinary person. She seemed to have figured out an approach to God that could be followed by anyone because it was so simple. She had taken to heart what Jesus said about whom we should resemble—a little child. Her "Little Way" of spiritual childhood promoted a new attitude of mind and heart in approaching God; it consisted in feeling and acting as a child feels and acts by nature. Thérèse knew that if she turned to God with the heart of a helpless child who goes to a generous father, who dotes on her and from whom she expects everything (which is exactly the sort of father she had in her natural life), he would always take care of her.

She believed that if God is a loving Father, he must also be a forgiving father. By admitting our sinfulness and weakness, we can, in a sense, turn our sins to our advantage. Consequently, the weakest sinners are able to see in her Little Way something especially for them. Although she didn't minimize the seriousness of sin, we should not let our sins crush us. The saints she most admired were not those known for great works, extraordinary mortifications or martyrdom. Rather, she delighted in those who "stole" heaven, so to speak, like the Good Thief. She wanted to be a thief and win it by a "stratagem—a stratagem of love which will open its gates to me and to poor sinners."

Thérèse's Little Way was nothing really new; she was simply following what Jesus taught us. What was different from the approach of other saints was her freshness and simplicity. She was able to make average men and women better understand what God expects of them. He doesn't look for great things—he already has greatness in abundance. He wants them to be themselves. If only they accept their littleness, their complete dependence on him, perfection comes within reach. Once they put away their haughty airs and accept, even revel in, their true position as his children, he delights in them just like any other father. They are able to conquer him by humility because by being humble they accept and rejoice in their true relationship to him. The more they admit and accept their littleness for love of him, the more room they leave for him to enter into them. Once they empty themselves of all pretensions, they are ready to be filled with him.

Thérèse's vocation was to love God, and her mission to make

millions of others love him as she loved him. Her point in developing a childlike attitude was not that this should be an end in itself, but rather that it was the necessary precondition that disposed one to do everything for love of God. She believed that little things done out of love charm the heart of Christ but the most brilliant deeds done without love are worth nothing. Once armed with blind dependency on God, everything in life becomes a means of expressing that love. The intention and love behind any act is what interests him.

Thérèse believed that Christ not only wants our love, but thirsts for it. In her autobiography she writes that he "wasn't ashamed to beg for a drop of water from the Samaritan woman—but then, he was thirsty, and thirsty for what? It was the love of this one despised creature that the Maker of heaven and earth asked for, when he said: 'Give me some to drink' [John 4: 7]; he was thirsty for love."[4] In a letter to her sister Céline she sees Christ as one who "stretches out His hand to us like a *beggar*... it is He who wants our love, *begs* for it. He puts Himself, so to say, at our mercy. He wills to take nothing unless we give it to Him, and the smallest thing is precious in His divine eyes... but He does not want us to love Him for His gifts; it is *Himself* that must be our *reward*."[5]

Thérèse's Little Way is so simple and direct anyone can follow it. No longer does sanctity depend on endless prayers and difficult acts of self-denial, unattainable except by a few. She puts it in reach of everyone. Her Way is not a system of prayer and it has no complicated rules; rather, it is based on principles that anyone can accept. And once accepted, each person can adapt them to his or her own personality and individual needs without having to fit into a common mold.

Long before Matt Talbot heard of Thérèse, he had already developed a childlike attitude towards God. When he later learned of her, he knew she was a kindred spirit—"a wonderful little girl," as he called her—whose Little Way best expressed where he wanted to go and how he planned to get there. He was among the first to contribute money—$5 from his meager wages—for the construction of a shrine in her honor in Dublin. He kept the prayer for her beatification among his few prized possessions and recited it daily. But much as Matt was enchanted with Thérèse, in his usual fashion of doing everything to excess he ignored her warnings against severe fasts and mortifications. No one—not even the Little Flower—would ever get him to give up his secret plank bed and wooden pillow or his chains.

Chapter XVI

Matt Talbot Today

God has a way of raising up saints according to the needs of the times. He often chooses the weak and unassuming in order to convince the rest of us that what was possible for them can be attained by anyone. All around we see abuse or outright addiction to alcohol and drugs. Is it not providential that the world has a working model in Matt Talbot—without his excesses of course—of how anyone can overcome addiction?

Whether the Catholic Church canonizes Matt as a saint is almost beside the point. A primary purpose of canonization is to provide the faithful with a hero for imitation. But Matt is already a hero to many alcoholics. They see in him proof that they can overcome their addiction. Anyway, the Church already recognizes him as a hero. In 1975, as the first major step towards canonization, it declared him to be "Venerable"—to be worthy of imitation because of the essential Christian quality of his life. However, it was not his wearing of chains, his sleeping on a plank bed or his continual fasts and endless prayers that are suggested for imitation. Indeed, chains and that sort of thing have been out of favor in the Church for some time and are even forbidden. Rather, it was the way he performed the ordinary, humdrum duties of everyday life so extraordinarily well and animated them with an ever-deepening love of God that makes him a person worthy of our imitation.

The Church does not recommend that the life of any saint be imitated slavishly, but it does suggest that there are elements in Matt's spiritual life anyone can draw upon in overcoming alcoholism and drug addiction. When Matt gave up drink, he began by doing what was quite common then—he took "the pledge"—a promise to abstain from alcoholic beverages with the help of God. (It is not suggested that followers of the Matt Talbot Way use pledges, promises, or vows in achieving sobriety, even though Matt may have been successful with this approach.) Although his pledge was a promise, it was not binding as a solemn vow would have been. In any event, Matt knew that if he was going to succeed in keeping it, a dedicated practice of his Catholic faith had to go with it. But leading just a good Catholic life was not enough for him. He started out slowly, gradually adding more and more prayers and austere practices to his daily routine; within a few years, we have the Matt Talbot now known to the world.

Underlying all his prayers and penitential practices was a childlike approach to God. Although the idea of spiritual childhood was the central teaching of St. Thérèse of Lisieux, it was not unique with her; it is a theme that runs through the lives of all the saints—something that Matt knew before he ever heard of Thérèse. But she expressed it more lucidly than anyone since Christ. Whether from her or others, or directly from the Gospels, Matt learned that if he put away the haughty airs that people tend to put on, and accepted, even reveled in, his true nature as a creature of God, a child of the Father, God in turn would take delight in him just like any other father. Matt lovingly accepted the reality of this Father-son relationship. He never forgot how drink had once laid him low, and that it was only the love of the Father for him as his son, and his response to that love, that gave him the power to lift himself up.

But Matt was not content to accept just a Father-son relationship, as though all was forgiven and forgotten as when the Prodigal Son returned home. The past weighed too heavily on Matt to be left behind so easily. Looking back on his life, he saw sixteen years devoted to drink, with no concern for the needs of his family or his own spiritual well-being. When he took the pledge, he went to his first confession in years. This should have been enough to wipe the slate clean, so to speak—but not for Matt. His inner lights demanded much more.

As he saw it, to set things in balance his life should take on a definite penitential character. Although he may have learned in time that unusual mortifications were at odds with the attitude of the holy nun from Lisieux whom he greatly admired, that did not matter to him in the least. What began as a trickle of prayers, fasts and other "little penances"—as when he gave up his pipe—became in time a steady stream of acts of self-denial, inexorably leading to his plank bed and ultimately to his chains, considering his natural tendency to do everything to excess.

Although Matt's motivation during the years right after he gave up drinking was to atone for the past, this gradually changed to a consuming desire to somehow become one with the crucified Christ. If Jesus suffered and died on the cross for love of him, it seemed only right that he should be willing to show his love and gratitude by taking on a few sacrifices of his own devising. It was this all-engrossing love, his desire to commiserate with the suffering Christ, that drove him to take on the chains and the rest.

In assessing his extraordinary penances and how today they might fit in with the Matt Talbot Way to sobriety, we find that they really do not fit at all. They were simply Matt's own way, peculiar to him. Once we understand this, they are best forgotten. Followers of the Matt Talbot Way who feel the need to take on special penances should look upon their continuing acts of doing without drink as the best penance. After all, Jesus answered the Pharisees' question as to why his disciples did not fast from food and drink like those of John the Baptist by saying, "they will fast in those days" when he was no longer with them (Luke 5:35).

Matt of course left no writings on penitential or any other matters so we have to look elsewhere to find a sense of balance and proportion. Saint Thérèse of Lisieux provides precisely this, though you would think that a girlish nun who lived her entire life completely sheltered from anything smacking of drink or drugs would be the last person to turn to. Matt may be the hero and model of the Matt Talbot Way but Thérèse has become in large measure its theologian. Indeed, in 1997 the Catholic Church named her a Doctor of Theology—one of only three woman saints ever so honored—thus giving its stamp of approval to her teaching as a simple and direct way to God.

Matt's chains and plank bed, his endless fasts and prayers, are simply out of harmony with Thérèse's teaching. Although the prevailing attitude in her convent was to admire saints who went in for bodily mortifications, she developed a deep mistrust of anything unusual for herself, as well as for those in her charge, for she was the mistress of novices. The basic rules of convent life were enough for her—she preferred the simple, ordinary, almost monotonous things of everyday life. It was enough for her to do these "little things" cheerfully, and to do them well, but most important, to do them for love of God. What concerned her was not so much the acts she did in his service, as the intention she brought to them and the love with which she animated them. She believed that the slightest movement of disinterested love was worth more in the eyes of God than the grandest acts in the eyes of man. The love of God was the only thing that really mattered—it was this that should motivate everything we do.

Spiritual childhood is not only for those who have retained their childhood innocence unsullied by sin. It is not some sort of exclusive privilege meant only for an elite. When Jesus said, "Unless you turn and become like children…" (Matthew 18:3), he presupposed a lost innocence that needed to be regained. Who can become like a child except someone who is no longer one? It is this availability of a childlike attitude to anyone who wants it—even to the most abject of sinners—that makes the Little Way so delightfully appealing. After all, all Christians are sinners, even "good" Christians. Sinners especially can learn how to apply it in their daily lives as they approach God and turn from their old ways. More than that, they are able to use it to transform individual acts of daily life into little acts of love for him. Things now done for love of him take on a life of their own and become the means of perpetuating themselves.

For these reasons Thérèse's Little Way has a natural appeal to alcoholics who follow the Matt Talbot Way. Once they recognize and accept their weakness for drink, they can turn it to their advantage by placing complete trust in God's love for them. Regardless of how low they may have fallen, they are able to respond with their own love. No longer will they use their weakness as an excuse to continue as before. They come to understand that God is always approachable and wants only their love. Finally, they are able to quit drinking solely for love of him. Each act of doing without drink—each an act of love of God—becomes the means to continue this never-ending series of acts of love. As they grow in love for God, the idea that they will ever stop loving him becomes unthinkable—they will never go back to drinking.

The drink they give up, however, is not something evil, though the way they used it may have become that. Quite the contrary: Alcoholic beverages of all types are among the singular delights of God's good world. Followers of the Matt Talbot Way should always look upon drink in the same way that St. Francis saw God's goodness and love reflected in all creation. It is precisely because of its essential goodness that drink is so worthy to be given up for love of him, though at the outset they may have doubts about this. In time, however, they will come to perceive drink for its intrinsic goodness, and that it is this that they choose to do without for love of Christ.

Whether in time the Church confers on Matt Talbot the full honors of sainthood depends on irrefutable proof of miraculous cures of a *physical* nature obtained through his intercession with God. The Church wants full medical proof of cures that come about in such an extraordinary fashion that the only possible explanation is the intervening hand of God. It cautiously looks for his seal of approval, so to speak, before it gives its own. But instead of wondering when and if these miracles will come about, followers of the Matt Talbot Way in their own quiet, hidden fashion are able to draw down a different kind of miracle. These may be only *spiritual* miracles perhaps, but to them, they are miracles nonetheless.

St. Thérèse explained this when, near the end of her life, she wrote: "'Give me a lever and a fulcrum,' said the man of science, 'and I'll shift the world.' Archimedes wasn't talking to God, so his request wasn't granted; and in any case he was only thinking of the material world. But the Saints really have enjoyed the privilege he asked for; the fulcrum God told them to use was himself, nothing less than himself, and the lever was prayer. Only it must be the kind of prayer that sets the heart all on fire with love."[1] Although Thérèse speaks of saints having this power with God, it is not something that belongs only to them. She would be the first to contend that by using the right stratagem, anyone can take it for his or her own, including alcoholics and drug addicts.

The Matt Talbot Way demands a pristine kind of love: Christ is loved for his own sake alone, with nothing being asked for or expected in return—not even the virtue of temperance. Followers pray that they may "learn to know and love [Jesus Christ] without measure." And once armed with that love, they offer to God each day the pleasures of alcohol solely for love of him. It is the purity of this love for Christ—love of God for its own sake—of which Thérèse speaks. Followers of the Matt Talbot Way make Christ the fulcrum; their love for him and the expression of that love—their daily gift of doing without the delights of drink—becomes their lever. They find a sure way to draw down a miracle of grace from God in attaining complete power over alcohol.

Matt mastered the old tyranny of drink over his body by doing what today's world will say is ridiculous. Some will even say, as in his time, that he must have been crazy. But when you reflect on what he wanted in life—to grow steadily in love of God—maybe he wasn't so crazy after all. Maybe it is the sober-minded people of the world, at least those who lack Matt's vision of love of God, who are able to do little more than stagger, at best, as they lurch towards him.

Perhaps God only wants us to understand how weak we are without him, and that it is often those who are insignificant in the eyes of the world who are best at finding him. Is it not more than just ironic that with the world's emphasis on money and possessions, power and position, a poor, uneducated workingman has become the perfect example of how anyone can overcome addiction to things of the world? Nothing much has changed with Matt: In his younger days as a bricklayers' laborer he was put out in front of his fellow workers to set the pace. Today he is still out in front, urging the rest of us on—"If I can do it, so can you!"

Part Three

Other Uses of the Matt Talbot Way

"Do you love me?" and [Peter] said to him,
"Lord, you know everything. You know that I love you."

John 21:18

XVII

Getting Off Cigarettes

Although the Matt Talbot Way is meant primarily for alcoholics and drug addicts, it can be a highly effective aid for smokers. Most smokers prefer to think that their attachment to cigarettes doesn't put them in the same class as alcoholics and drug addicts, but the reality is that they are addicted, to a greater or lesser degree, to nicotine, which is a drug. In fact, nicotine is one of the most addicting drugs known. Many smokers have found that it is harder for them to give up cigarettes than for drug addicts to get off hard drugs or for alcoholics to give up booze. Nevertheless, in deference to their squeamishness about being categorized as drug addicts, smokers are treated here in a class by themselves; to be fair, though, smokers do have somewhat different hurdles to clear than users of hard drugs.

If you have zeroed in on this chapter hoping to find a shortcut to quitting, you will be disappointed. In fact, you will find no program here at all. If you are going to be successful in getting off cigarettes, you will probably need a program along the lines of those proposed by the American Cancer Society, the American Lung Association and the American Heart Association.[1] By following such guidelines you can design a program that will best satisfy what you perceive to be your precise needs.

Tens of millions of American smokers have been able to quit, but most of them had to go through several tries at giving them up before they were able to say they had quit for good. So it only makes sense to design your personal program to take advantage of these successes (and failures), as do the suggested guidelines of the American Cancer Society et al. And if you add to your program that of the Matt Talbot Way (as adapted for smokers), getting off will not only be easier and more certain, but in the end, far more satisfying. It can spell the difference between success and failure. Like going hunting with a shotgun, you want both barrels loaded and ready. In any event, though, the routine of the Matt Talbot Way won't interfere in any way with whatever program you devise to stop smoking.

Here are the basic approaches to quitting: You can devise a do-it-yourself plan. Or you can go the route of a group support program or find individual counseling, all of which will help you to cope with the problems that develop as you begin to do without cigarettes. To boost your chance of success, you may want to get assistance from nicotine replacement products, such as a nicotine patch or nicotine gum (both can be obtained over-the-counter), or from a nicotine nasal spray or nicotine inhaler (both require a doctor's prescription). These will help you contend with withdrawal, particularly during the initial period after quitting. According to the American Lung Association, smokers who use some sort of nicotine substitute and participate in a change of behavior program (such as following their 7 Steps to a Smoke-Free Life) can double their likelihood of success.

Another approach to help smokers wean themselves off nicotine are non-nicotine prescription drugs. Zyban, for example, an antidepressant drug that has long been prescribed by doctors under the trade name Wellbutrin SR, acts on the brain to give a sense of energy and well being, the same feelings as produced by nicotine.

When you begin your program to get off cigarettes, you can stop "cold turkey," quitting completely the day you have set to begin—your start date. Some smokers may simply wake up one morning—maybe after a night of bad coughing—and decide on the spot they have had enough and are going to quit without further ado. While their initial motivation may be very strong, a more deliberate approach usually gives better results.

But for many smokers the prospect of abruptly doing without cigarettes is so frightening they can't bring themselves to consider it seriously. To lessen this problem, you can go through a process of "nicotine fading" in which you switch to cigarette brands with lower and lower nicotine content, even though you continue to smoke your regular number of cigarettes a day. In this way you gradually reduce your addiction to nicotine *before* the arrival of your start date.

Going through a process of nicotine fading works particularly well in conjunction with the Matt Talbot Way, which also requires a period of preparation before the start date. But to follow the Matt Talbot Way you have to have a full understanding of it. Essentially, you have to go through the same process as an alcoholic or hard drug addict does in getting off drink and/or drugs the Matt Talbot Way. This means that you must read the entire book *like a handbook*, from the Preface through Chapter XVI, assimilating everything slowly. If you simply skim it, trying to pick up a few points here and there, hoping to catch its essence, you won't begin to fully and deeply understand the workings of the Way. You can't expect it to work under these conditions. However, once you have read the entire book carefully, you can go about integrating it with the program you have settled on for getting off cigarettes—the start date will be the same for both.

Whether your doctor has told you that cigarettes are killing you and you had better quit, you have a terrible cough and feel lousy most of the time, you have come to realize that second-hand smoke is a danger to your family and everyone around you, or whatever your motivations might be, these by themselves may not be strong enough to keep you off cigarettes. However, adding the potent motivation of the Matt Talbot Way to your worldly ones could make the difference between getting off cigarettes for good and another courageous struggle that ends in failure.

To add the Matt Talbot Way, you have to follow the seven steps set out in detail in Chapter VI, but as adapted for use by smokers rather than alcoholics. Whether in giving up alcohol or hard drugs, or as an aid to giving up cigarettes, with the Matt Talbot Way you must pursue a strategy based upon love of Jesus Christ. By focusing your love upon him, you are able to develop a *positive* motivation that may be much stronger than all the *negative* motivations you have for quitting, no matter how valid these may be. With this two-track motivational approach, you attack your attachment to cigarettes with the greatest possible force.

To quit smoking the Matt Talbot Way you make a complete gift of yourself and all your actions to God each day. In particular, you offer him whatever pleasure you find in cigarettes, not by smoking as in the past, but by choosing to do without them *as an express act of love for his son, Jesus Christ*. To be able to begin doing this on your start date, you have to prepare yourself by following all seven steps of the Matt Talbot Way. You can't just decide one day that you've had enough of smoking and that now you are going to quit the Matt Talbot Way. Like nicotine fading, you have to prepare yourself. In particular, you must follow the third step of the Way by praying in a regular and systematic Christ-centered fashion.

As part of step one of the Way, during the preparation period before your start each day, you make the following Daily Offering to God each morning:

> Heavenly Father, being mindful of the heroic example of your servant Matt Talbot, I offer you during this day myself, all my works and prayers, joys and sorrows, as an expression of love for your Son, Jesus Christ. I pray that these gifts may be pleasing to you, and that you will favor me with your blessings, through the same Christ, our Lord. Amen.

When your start day arrives, however, you permanently add to the Daily Offering, after the words "joys and sorrows" and before the words "as an expression," the following words:

> "and, in particular, the pleasures and delights of cigarettes, which I forgo,"

You should make the Daily Offering immediately upon waking, since it is the spiritual focal point of each day and provides that extra dimension, purpose and direction in your desire to quit smoking that can make the difference. To be able to say the prayer, particularly after your start date, will depend on regular and systematic prayer that centers on the person of Jesus Christ, as well as following all the other steps of the Way.

Once you have gone through the initial phase of quitting,

cigarettes usually won't have the same appeal for you as the lifelong attraction that alcohol has for alcoholics. Nevertheless, doing without cigarettes each day can be a continuing act of love for God that you can renew each day for the rest of your life.

Looking down the road, if you are like many people, you may gain a few pounds because your body is burning calories more slowly as it adjusts to being nicotine-free. Just don't let that become an excuse to even think you might want to start smoking again. Any weight gain will be much less of a threat to your health than the cigarettes. In any event, your continued following of the Matt Talbot Way will make it much easier to stay off them.

Maybe you never had to think about weight control or dieting before, but now you find yourself hoping that every new diet that comes along will have the answer. However, in the Matt Talbot Way you already have a solution. Yes, you should follow sound principles of nutrition and you should exercise. But the discipline required for avoiding unwanted weight gain or the loss of a few pounds can also be found in the Way. And in many ways it can be far more effective and satisfying than any diet. For this, be sure to read Chapter XVIII, Controlling Your Weight.

XVIII

Controlling Your Weight

Having read nearly all of *To Slake a Thirst*, you may feel somehow left out if you don't have a problem with alcohol, don't take drugs or don't smoke. You may wonder, isn't there some way you can benefit from the Matt Talbot Way? You can triumph over a variety of addictions using the Matt Talbot Way—that is, by increasing your love for Jesus Christ. This should be the aim of all Christians of course.

With all the talk about dieting, sometimes it seems as though everyone you know worries about their weight and what they can do to control it. Whether you are only a few pounds overweight or fat, you probably would like to weigh close to what you did in your 20's. Or if you don't think of yourself as being overweight now, you know that if you don't watch it, with the passage of a few years it could well become a problem. And once you put on those extra pounds, they are not easy to get rid of. All you have to do is look around you the next time you go to a restaurant to see the great number of people who haven't done much to avoid the problem.

Although the Matt Talbot Way is meant primarily for alcoholics, the same technique that gives them power over liquor can be adapted to give you control over what you eat, enabling you over time to either lose unwanted weight or to avoid putting it on in the first place. Since weight control can be a lifelong problem, it demands a lifelong solution. With the Way, you will not only be able to exert a high degree of control over your weight for the rest of your life (not including serious illness of course), but as part of that same process you will grow in love for God.

Being overweight certainly doesn't put you in the same class as alcoholics; nevertheless, the underlying cause of the problem is almost always much the same: you have become too attached to the good things of this world—you eat too much for your level of physical activity, so you put on weight.

One often hears that diets don't work, that people who go on them always wind up gaining back whatever initial weight loss they are able to achieve—and then some. But the problem may not be so much with the diet as with the dieter who follows it only halfheartedly. Dieters tend to find little ways to go off their diet, rationalizing that such little slips can't really make much difference. While each such variance may be small and add only what seems like a few calories, the sheer number of slips may be enough to do much violence to the diet they claim to be following. So they don't lose weight or they gain back whatever they do lose.

With the Matt Talbot Way you won't find the magic diet that everyone seems to be looking for: eat as much as you want of your favorite foods and still lose weight. In fact, you won't find listed here any diet at all. Rather, you have complete control in selecting the diet you want to follow. And if you are not satisfied with the first one, find another. But that doesn't mean that you should follow any fad diet that comes along. Whatever you select should be a fairly well-balanced diet that, with modifications, can become your weight maintenance diet—at that point, of course, it isn't really a "diet" at all—that you should follow the rest of your life. Also, keep in mind that regular exercise should be an integral part of your weight control program—both during the dieting phase and during weight maintenance.

But regardless of the diet you follow, the Matt Talbot Way shows you how to develop the power to say no each time you are tempted to go off your diet. To prepare yourself to follow the Way requires a careful reading of *To Slake a Thirst*, from the Preface through Chapter XVI. To do this most effectively, put yourself in the shoes of an alcoholic—the Way is meant primarily for him—and read the entire book with the same hope and enthusiasm that he must have if he is to find a way to give up liquor for good (but without remaining powerless in doing so), and do it all for the love of God. When you have finished reading, ideally you should almost regret that you are not an alcoholic, thinking you would like to be able to give up something you are so attached to for love of Jesus Christ. Now you are ready to follow the Way, as adapted for weight control.

The heart of the Way is in Chapter VI, The Matt Talbot Way. You must follow the seven steps, from praying in a regular, Christ-centered fashion to daily spiritual reading and all the other steps. But there are slight differences when compared to the Way for an alcoholic. In making your Daily Offering to God each day, nothing is said about giving up alcohol or drugs (or cigarettes, for that matter). Instead, you add the words, "and in particular, the pleasures and delights of the food and drink I choose to do without."

> Heavenly Father, being mindful of the heroic example of your servant Matt Tatbot, I offer you during this day

myself, all my works and prayers, joys and sorrows, and in particular, the pleasures and delights of the food and drink I choose to do without, as an expression of love for your Son, Jesus Christ. I pray that these gifts may be pleasing to you, and that you will favor me with your blessings, through the same Christ, our Lord. Amen.

With this prayer you express your complete trust in God by accepting whatever the day might bring, and then freely offer that back to him as a gift of love. There is no mention of giving up certain foods or how much you eat, etc., or for that matter, any reference to the rules or requirements of whatever diet you might choose to follow. But now to your worldly motivation in cutting down on how much you eat and drink, you have added the powerful other-worldly motivation of doing so as an express act of love for Jesus Christ. To be sure, your primary motivation will almost certainly be those worldly concerns, but the combination of the two motivations makes the job so much easier.

When you go on a diet you generally know which foods are permissible and which are not, in what combinations and portions, what snacks are permitted, etc. Although most people start out with the best of intentions, hewing closely to the diet for a week or so, usually with some success, they often become bored with it and are only too ready to bend its rules, reasoning that such minor rule breaking won't make that much difference. But the cumulative effect is often enough to stop any further weight loss.

By joining the Matt Talbot Way to your diet, however, you will be surprised at the strength you have to pass up that piece of candy—or whatever else you find especially tempting—in situations where in the past you almost certainly would have given in. You will be able to do this because you are making a gift of your enjoyment of the candy to God as an expression of your love for his Son, Jesus Christ. The first time you are able to do this, you will know right then that you are well on your way to controlling your weight through the Matt Talbot Way (assuming that your weight problem comes from eating too much and is not glandular in nature). Using the same technique, you will be able to resist breaking the rules of your diet in countless ways: avoiding non-permissible foods and second helpings, taking the proper size portions, snacking only as permitted by the diet, etc. Now, when you are tempted to bend a rule, even slightly, you have a newfound power to say no. And each victory over yourself, even in such a small matter, gives you added strength, both spiritually and psychologically, for the next time.

Your initial motivation for saying no comes, of course, from your desire to lose weight; the difference now, however, is that you are able to say no unfailingly because of the power unleashed by the Matt Talbot Way, and through it, your desire to express your love for Christ, even in small ways. You will be able to do this many times each day. Actually, you may find yourself looking for ways to express that love as you follow your diet. When an alcoholic follows the Matt Talbot Way, he works up to making a big, one-time decision to say no to alcohol, which he then reaffirms every day; the dieter following the Way makes only very small decisions during the day about what he chooses to eat or not eat for love of Christ.

This is not to say that every decision in following your diet must be centered on the Way, only that when you are tempted to bend the diet's rules in an unacceptable way do you need to rely on the special power that comes from following it. Indeed, you don't ordinarily want to get into the habit of following the Way in a robotic fashion, thinking, for example, that you must avoid certain foods without fail. Depending on the severity of your weight problem, how strict you want to be with yourself, and the timetable you have set for yourself, it's best not to be too demanding of yourself. Although it has been emphasized here that the easy and regular bending of the rules of a diet leads to its failure, nevertheless, when you diet in conjunction with the Matt Talbot Way, a selective breaking of the diet's rules is not necessarily a bad thing. By easing up on yourself at times and even giving in, you are able to satisfy to a degree your craving for certain foods, which in the end, may help you stay on the diet. The important point is that with the Way, even though you give in from time to time, you have complete control over such deviations and are able to place limits on their future occurrence.

At some point you should achieve the body weight you have set for yourself—assuming your goal is realistic. When that happens, you should be able to maintain your new weight with good eating habits. That does not mean, however, that you will no longer need the Matt Talbot Way. In fact, you will need it particularly when you find yourself digressing continually from good eating habits, which almost certainly will lead to gaining back some or all of the weight you went to so much trouble to lose. It's at this point where the Way can be vital in keeping you in line.

So when you stop "dieting" as such, and change over to a weight maintenance program—which is simply the sum of good eating habits you should follow for the rest of your life—it's important to continue following all seven steps of the Matt Talbot Way. By doing so, when you need it for added strength to avoid going too far afield from your new eating program, it will be there. Actually, once you bring your weight under control, you probably will find that you *want* to continue following the Way, irrespective of how much it can help you to maintain your weight. You will probably find yourself looking for ways to express your love for Christ every day, by denying yourself some food that you particularly like. Weight control will now be a pleasant side effect of the Way, and you will follow it because it's a wonderful, even handy, way to express your love for God.

Even if you aren't overweight, the Matt Talbot Way can help keep you that way. Being overweight may not yet be a problem for you, but quite probably as you grow older you will begin to put on pounds; older people need less food, but they tend to eat the same amount. By following an eating program based on good eating habits, in conjunction with the seven steps of the Way, they can keep from gaining the extra weight to begin with and may never need to actually diet.

And if you are one of those favored people who have never had a weight problem, and probably never will, you don't have to feel left out; although you may not need the Matt Talbot Way to control your weight, you can still take advantage of it to express your love for God. By tapping into the Way, you can not only learn to control your weight, but you can actually increase your love for Jesus Christ.

The initial reaction of some people to the Way as adapted for weight control, is that it's just too easy. Unless you do something much more demanding than giving up a little food from time to time, even though given expressly for love of Jesus Christ, can such "gifts" have much value in the sight of God? However, we should keep in mind that we tend to take the good things of the world for granted; the food that comes to us daily should be a constant reminder of God's love and generosity. Since God gives us all these good things, why shouldn't food—especially food we are fond of—be a fit object for us to show our love for him by occasionally denying ourselves its enjoyment?

St. Thérèse of Lisieux taught that to please God we can and should do everything in life for love, even the "tiniest" things. Doing without food from time to time, and doing it for love of God, fits in well with her philosophy. (Reread Chapters XV and XVI.) St. Thérèse wrote that "little things done out of love are those that charm the Heart of Christ... the most brilliant deeds, when done without love, are but nothingness."[1] But some would say that making a gift to God of food that you choose to do without is not a completely pure gift to start with, in that you have an ulterior motive—you want to control your weight. To a degree, this is true. Nevertheless, there is a substantial element of a gift; in fact, without the power which you find by following the Way, in many such situations you wouldn't be able to make the gift at all—you would choose to eat the food. So don't look to your imperfections or the imperfections of your gifts; but like Thérèse, trust that God will lovingly accept whatever you give back to him.

St. Paul said it best: "Whatever you eat, then, or drink, and whatever else you do, do it all for the glory of God" (1 Cor 10: 30-31). Thus, what you choose not to eat as you follow the Way can be an expression of that love, regardless of whether your primary reason for doing so may be your quite worldly concern about how much you weigh.

SELECTED WRITINGS ABOUT MATT TALBOT

John Beevers. "Matt Talbot," *Shining as Stars*. Westminster, MD: Newman Press, 1956.

Malachy Gerard Carroll. *The Story of Matt Talbot*. Cork, Ireland: Mercier Press, 1948.

James F. Cassidy. *Matt Talbot: The Irish Worker's Glory*. Dublin: Burns, Oates & Washbourne, 1934.

Morgan Costelloe. *The Mystery of Matt Talbot*. Dublin: Irish Messenger Publications, 1981.

———. *Matt Talbot—Hope for Addicts*. Dublin: Veritas Publications, 1987.

Eddie Doherty. *Matt Talbot*. Milwaukee: Bruce Publishing Company, 1953.

Albert H. Dolan. *Matt Talbot, Alcoholic*. Englewood, NJ: The Carmelite Press, 1947.

Sir Joseph A. Glynn. *Life of Matt Talbot*. Dublin: Catholic Truth Society of Ireland, 1942.

Edward O'Connor. *Spotlight on the Venerable Matt Talbot*. Dublin: Irish Messenger Publications, 1977.

Mary Purcell. *Matt Talbot and His Times*. Chicago: Franciscan Herald Press, 1977.

———. *The Making of Matt Talbot*. Dublin: Irish Messenger Publications, 1972.

———. *Remembering Matt Talbot*. Dublin: Veritas Publications, 1990.

F.J. Sheed. "Matt Talbot," F.J. Sheed, ed., *The Irish Way*. New York: Sheed & Ward, 1934.

Appendices

Appendix I

Summary of the Matt Talbot Way

The Matt Talbot Way to sobriety is a stratagem based upon love: By systematically praying to increase your love for Jesus Christ, a time will come when you will be able to give up the pleasures of alcohol simply for love of him. To bring this about, your faith and love must grow. For this, you must pray in a regular and methodical fashion. You do this by following the seven steps of the Way every day.

1. Daily Offering

Immediately upon awakening, you express your love for God through the Daily Offering by choosing to do without the pleasures of alcohol:

Daily Offering

Heavenly Father, being mindful of the heroic example of your servant Matt Talbot, I offer you during this day myself, all my works and prayers, joys and sorrows, and in particular, the worldly pleasures and delights of alcohol [or drugs or whatever else you are attached to but have decided to give up], which I forgo, as an expression of love for your son, Jesus Christ. I pray that these gifts may be pleasing to you, and that you will favor me with your blessing, through the same Christ, our Lord. Amen.

To be able to recite the complete prayer, however, including the words "and in particular, the worldly pleasures and delights of alcohol which I forgo," you must follow the other steps of the Way. You must pray systematically to develop the depth of love on which everything else depends. But if you follow the Way with a steady resolve, a time will come when your love for God will have grown sufficiently for you to quit drinking. Until then, when making the Daily Offering you should omit these words.

2. Christ-Centered Prayer

At the heart of the Way is prayer centered on Jesus Christ. With this step you pray that your mind may be open to Christ so as to allow him to enter into your heart. When you pray with this single-minded objective, your love will increase to the point where you will be able to give up drink solely for the love of him.

One of the best Christ-centered prayers is the Jesus Prayer—"Lord Jesus Christ, Son of God, have mercy on me, a sinner." You should say this prayer thoughtfully and silently at least one hundred times each day. Many find it effective to synchronize the prayer with the natural rhythm of breathing. Although there may be other Christ-centered prayers that you will come to prefer, you will probably find this is the best to begin with. Later you may substitute others if you wish. If you are a Catholic, read Appendix II for Christ-centered prayers with which you should be familiar and which are more attuned to Matt Talbot's actual method of prayer.

3. Dedication of the Prayers of the Day

After praying the main body of your Christ-centered prayers for the day, immediately say the Prayer to the Holy Spirit. This prayer gives purpose and direction to what you are trying to accomplish through the other steps, particularly the second—that your love for Jesus Christ may grow "without measure." In your prayers you do not ask God to keep you from drinking or even to give you the virtue of temperance; rather, your sole objective is to grow in love for Jesus Christ.

Prayer to the Holy Spirit
O Holy Spirit, may I receive Jesus Christ into my heart through you. Even as Mary his mother did, may I learn to know and love him without measure as Lord and Savior. Draw me to him so that I may imitate him in all things and thereby obtain the blessing of my heavenly Father, through the same Christ, our Lord. Amen.

In place of the above prayer, and more in keeping with Catholic tradition and the attitude of Matt Talbot, Catholic followers of the Way will probably want to substitute the following prayer, though either version may be used.

An Appeal to the Mother of God
O Blessed Mother of God, I beg you that I may receive your Son, Jesus, into my heart, through the Holy Spirit by whom you conceived him. Teach me to know and love him without measure, as you adore him as Lord and Savior. Draw me to him so that I may imitate him in all things and thereby obtain the blessing of our heavenly Father, through the same Christ, our Lord. Amen.

4. Spiritual Reading

If you are to grow spiritually, you must systematically build a foundation of knowledge to nourish your faith and ultimately your prayers. Ten or fifteen minutes a day should be spent in spiritual reading, with emphasis on the Bible, particularly the New Testament. Lives of Christ and the saints are also a good source.

5. Short Prayers during the Day

We tend to take the good things of the world for granted. You should look for ways to remind yourself in very short, simple prayers that you are his creature, and all good things of life depend upon him. *Grace* before dinner is an example of this.

Important though Christ-centered prayers are, you should look beyond the regular ones you say for other occasions of prayer during the day. To round out the prayers of the day, Catholics, for example, may want to silently pray the *Angelus* about midday. Also, praying at about three o'clock in the afternoon the *Prayer to the Crucified Christ* is a good way to remember the crucifixion of Jesus.

6. Evening prayer

Evening prayers may be very brief, though you may want to rededicate your prayers of the day to your main objective of growing in love for Jesus Christ.

7. Christian Living

An essential part of the Way is adherence to generally recognized Christian norms of living. The demands of Church and society must also be heeded. You are not expected to be perfect, only that you dispose yourself to try to lead a Christian life.

Appendix II

Christ-Centered Prayers for Catholics

THE HEART OF THE MATT TALBOT WAY IS THE SECOND STEP—Christ-centered prayer. With prayer that centers on the person of Jesus, you will have the desired growth in your love of him. Without that, you are not going to be willing or able to give up drink for love of him.

It is not suggested that you should incorporate all of the following prayers or methods of prayer into your third step. But they are among the very best to draw upon in developing your own routine. And it is crucial that you have a routine, that you know precisely what you are demanding of yourself every day. You should memorize the prayers you settle on, except, of course, the Mass. It will probably take considerable time to memorize all the prayers you settle upon, and you will not be able to memorize them all at once; take as much time as you need and do it by degrees. Soon enough, you will have them all memorized.

How you might go about deciding what prayers to select is discussed at the end of this appendix.

1. Daily Mass and Holy Communion

The Mass is the centerpiece of Catholic spiritual life, the perfect prayer of praise, adoration, petition and thanksgiving. And by receiving Holy Communion, not only does Christ truly come to you, but you are able to become present to him in his passion two thousand years ago. Part of his agony was on account of sins that were yet in the future but still foreseen by him; but the supplications and prayers of Christians were also foreseen and were a comfort and encouragement to him in his agony. As a follower of the Matt Talbot Way, you have a special opportunity to comfort him in his agony by bringing with you your uniquely personal balm—the gift of love for the suffering Christ expressed by your willingness to forgo the delights of alcohol.

2. Visits to the Blessed Sacrament

After Mass, the consecrated hosts that have not been consumed in Holy Communion are reserved in the tabernacle as the Blessed Sacrament. There, Jesus Christ remains truly present, waiting for those who can spend a few minutes with him in silent adoration and love, or just plain friendship, as they visit the church during the day.

Each visit to the Blessed Sacrament is an opportunity to grow in love for Christ. By spending a few moments of intimate friendship with him, you invite him to live in your heart in a more vital way. You cannot help but be drawn closer to him. If you do not have time for Mass in the morning, a visit during the day is a way to become spiritually refreshed, just as though you had received Christ in Holy Communion.

3. The Rosary

Not everyone has the time to go to Mass every day, but praying the rosary can be easily incorporated into your daily routine; it takes essentially no time away from your other activities. For most Catholics this will be the most practical centerpiece of their Christ-centered prayer.

The rosary is a Christ-centered prayer that is a perfect companion to reading the Gospels. It is an effective way to recall the story of the life, passion, death, and resurrection of Jesus, as seen through the eyes of the one who was closest to him, his mother. There is no better way for you to reflect on the life of Christ. You can easily integrate the rosary with those daily activities that do not require total concentration. To pray five of the fifteen "mysteries" of the rosary takes about fifteen minutes of your time.

The essence of the rosary is the quiet, rhythmic flow of the Hail Marys, coupled with devout reflection on Jesus, his life, and beyond. As you silently say the Hail Marys and your fingers pass over the beads (or as you use your fingers to count) you simultaneously meditate on the individual events of Jesus' life. It is a relatively free form of prayer; one moment you may be concentrating on the words of the Hail Mary itself, and the next your mind flashes to the Crucifixion, or the Resurrection, or whatever mystery you are meditating upon, and then back to the words again.

Whether you are walking, jogging, driving an automobile, riding a bus or train, or engaged in any other largely mechanical or repetitious activity, you can easily integrate the rosary with these actions. Although you ordinarily use beads when praying the rosary, this is not easily done when engaged in such activities as jogging or walking down a crowded street. While going about your more open activities, you can count the prayers on your fingers. In any event, in praying the rosary as well as following the other steps of the way, you should make no outward display.

Why pray the rosary in the first place? Because Mary is the perfect model to imitate in loving Jesus. She is the one whom Catholics and some other Christians naturally turn to for help in increasing that love. When you pray the rosary, you are doing essentially what she did. Luke tells us that Mary "kept all these things, pondering them in her heart," and again, that she "kept all these things in her heart" (Luke 2:19 and 2:51). After the Ascension of Jesus, she no doubt continued to reflect on all the events of his life, turning over in her mind what they meant for her and for the rest of us. It is no exaggeration to say that she was the first to pray the rosary, in a strictly limited sense of course, though not with the prayers or form of our present rosary—certainly she used no beads. By praying the rosary, you join her across the expanse of time and become a participant in spirit with her at the key events of Jesus' life.

4. *The Chaplet of Divine Mercy*

Also prayed on rosary beads, though it takes less time to say than five decades of the rosary, the Chaplet of Divine Mercy is an excellent way to foster love for Jesus Christ.

To pray the Chaplet, using rosary beads (or your fingers if you have no beads) first pray the Apostle's Creed, an Our Father and a Hail Mary. Then on the large beads (of which there are five) pray:

> Eternal Father, I offer You the Body and Blood, Soul and Divinity of Your dearly beloved Son, Our Lord Jesus Christ, in atonement for our sins and those of the whole world.

This is to be followed immediately ten times on the ten smaller beads with the following:

> For the sake of His sorrowful Passion have mercy on us and on the whole world.

All of this is repeated in this same fashion on the other four sets of beads. Thus, you pray the "Eternal Father…" prayer a total of five times and the "For the sake of…" prayer a total of fifty times. You finish the Chaplet by saying three times:

> Holy God, Holy Might One, Holy Immortal One, have mercy on us and on the whole world.

5. *The Angelus*

The Angelus recounts the angel Gabriel's message to Mary that she was chosen to become the mother of Jesus. Taken largely from a few verses of Luke and John, it is one of the most beautiful of all prayers. You should never tire of retelling the story of that awesome, yet delicate, moment. Like a mini-rosary, the whole expanse of our Redemption is recalled, from the message to Mary and her consent to be the mother of Jesus, to "his Passion and Cross… to the glory of his Resurrection." Traditionally, it is said at sunrise, noon and sunset.

The Angelus

> The Angel of the Lord declared unto Mary, and she conceived of the Holy Spirit.
> Hail Mary, full of grace, the Lord is with you. Blessed are you among women, and blessed is the fruit of your womb, Jesus.

Holy Mary, Mother of God, pray for us sinners, now and at the hour of our death. Amen.
Behold the handmaid of the Lord, be it done to me according to your word.
Hail Mary, full of grace…
And the Word was made flesh, and dwelt amongst us.
Hail Mary, full of grace…
Pray for us, O Holy Mother of God, that we may be made worthy of the promises of Christ.
Let us pray: Pour forth, we beseech thee, O Lord, thy grace into our hearts, that we, to whom the Incarnation of Christ thy Son was made known by the message of an angel, may by his Passion and Cross, be brought to the glory of his Resurrection, through the same Christ our Lord. Amen.

6. *Litany of the Sacred Heart*

The Litany of the Sacred Heart is possibly the finest Christ-centered prayer. It consists of a long series of invocations addressed to Jesus Christ which underscore that in his single person he has a fully developed human nature united with his divine nature. His Heart is looked upon as the symbol of his total Person, representing his boundless divine and human love for all—a love which in obedience to his Father culminated in his death on the cross and his heart being pierced with a lance.

The prayer is quite lengthy, but it takes only a few minutes to pray and meditate upon. You should memorize it (as with all your regular Christ-centered prayers), though at first this may appear to be quite a formidable task; with a little persistence, you will find that it's not that difficult.

Lord, have mercy.
Christ, have mercy.
Lord, have mercy.
Christ, hear us.
Christ, graciously hear us.
God, the Father of Heaven, have mercy on us.
God the Son, Redeemer of the world, have mercy on us.
God the Holy Spirit, have mercy on us.
Holy Trinity, one God, have mercy on us.
Heart of Jesus, Son of the eternal Father, have mercy on us.
Heart of Jesus, formed by the Holy Spirit in the Womb of the Virgin Mother,
Heart of Jesus, united hypostatically to the Word of God,
Heart of Jesus, of infinite majesty,
Heart of Jesus, Temple of God,
Heart of Jesus, Tabernacle of the Most High,
Heart of Jesus, House of God and Gate of heaven,
Heart of Jesus, burning furnace of charity,
Heart of Jesus, abode of justice and love,
Heart of Jesus, full of goodness and love,
Heart of Jesus, abyss of all virtue,
Heart of Jesus, most worthy of all praise,
Heart of Jesus, King and center of all hearts,
Heart of Jesus, in whom are all the treasures of wisdom and knowledge,
Heart of Jesus, in whom dwells all the fullness of the Godhead,
Heart of Jesus, in whom the Father is well pleased,
Heart of Jesus, of whose fullness we have all received,
Heart of Jesus, the desire of the everlasting hills,
Heart of Jesus, patient and full of mercy,

Heart of Jesus, rich to all who call on Thee,
Heart of Jesus, source of life and holiness,
Heart of Jesus, atonement for our sins,
Heart of Jesus, filled with reproaches,
Heart of Jesus, bruised for our sins,
Heart of Jesus, obedient even unto death,
Heart of Jesus, pierced with a lance,
Heart of Jesus, source of all consolation,
Heart of Jesus, our life and resurrection,
Heart of Jesus, our peace and reconciliation,
Heart of Jesus, victim for our sins,
Heart of Jesus, salvation of those who trust in Thee,
Heart of Jesus, hope of those who die in Thee,
Heart of Jesus, delight of all the saints,
Have mercy on us (after each).
Lamb of God, who takes away the sins of the world, spare us, O Lord.
Lamb of God, who takes away the sins of the world, graciously hear us, O Lord.
Lamb of God, who takes away the sins of the world, have mercy on us, O Lord.
Jesus, meek and humble of heart;
make my heart like unto Thine.

Let us pray: Almighty and eternal God, look on the Heart of Your most beloved Son and upon the praise and satisfaction He offers You in the name of sinners, and through their merit grant pardon to those who implore Your mercy in the name of your Son, Jesus Christ, who lives and reigns with You, world without end. Amen.

7. Stations of the Cross

All Catholic churches have fourteen crosses with plaques or statuary that depict scenes from Christ's passion and death. These Stations of the Cross represent the stops that pilgrims to the Holy Land make as they retrace the steps of Jesus as he carried his cross.

When you make the Stations of the Cross, you walk along with Jesus. You become like the disciples who followed him from a safe distance, although like Simon of Cyrene, you may choose to help him to carry the cross. As a vicarious participant, you begin to feel in your heart not only the sufferings of our Lord, but how great his love for you must have been for him to work your salvation in such an extraordinary fashion. With your heightened feelings and better understanding come a greater love for him.

The Stations of the Cross are ordinarily made at special services on Fridays during Lent. As the priest moves from station to station, the congregation follows him in prayer:

> We adore you, O Christ, and we praise you,
> Because by your holy cross you have redeemed the world.

Each station ends with a short discourse and a brief prayer.

The Stations of the Cross, however, are not just for Lent—they can be made any time. When followed privately in church, you walk from station to station as you meditate and pray according to your ability and available time. There are no fixed prayers required. A private praying of the Stations of the Cross need not even be in a church. You can follow Christ simply by holding or looking upon a crucifix while moving mentally from station to station and meditating upon his Passion. You may add other prayers of your choice, of course.

8. The Jesus Prayer

The Jesus Prayer has a long history going back to the early centuries of the Church. For the early Christians, particularly in the East, it was a way to pray ceaselessly. Today it is especially well-known to Orthodox Christians; but many others say it repeatedly as a simple and direct way to raise their minds and hearts to Jesus.

As you repeatedly pray the Jesus Prayer, "Lord Jesus Christ, Son of God, have mercy on me, a sinner," your mind should be directed to the single thought of the God-Man, Jesus Christ, both in his humanity and his divinity. You should say it from the heart slowly at least one hundred times each day. Particularly effective is the synchronization of the prayer with the natural rhythm of your breathing. There is no special magic to the precise number of times you say it, but by praying it repeatedly, you express the extent of your commitment to Christ.

9. Other Christ-Centered Prayers

The Loving Prayer

My God I love Thee,
Not because I hope
For heaven thereby.
Nor yet because
Who love Thee not
Are lost eternally.
Thou, O my Jesus, Thou didst me
Upon the cross embrace.
For me didst bear the nails and spear
And manifold disgrace.
And griefs and torments numerous

And sweat of agony.
Even death itself, and
All for one who was Thy enemy.
Then why, O Blessed Jesu Christi,
Should I not love Thee well.
Not for the sake of
Winning heaven or escaping hell
Not with the hope of gaining aught,
Not seeking a reward
But as Thyself has loved me
O ever loving Lord.
Even so, I love Thee
And will love and
In Thy praise will sing,
Solely because Thou art my God,
My everlasting King.
        (Attributed to St. Francis Xavier)

Prayer to the Crucified Christ

Look down upon me O good and gentle Jesus,
While before Thy face I humbly kneel,
And with burning soul pray and beseech thee
To fix deep in my heart
Lively sentiments of faith, hope and charity,
True contrition for my sins,
And a firm purpose of amendment.
While I contemplate with great love and tender pity
Thy five wounds,
Recalling the words which David the prophet spoke of You:

They have pierced My hands and My feet;
They have numbered all My bones.

Anima Christi

> Soul of Christ, be my sanctification,
> Body of Christ, be my salvation,
> Blood of Christ, fill all my veins,
> Water of Christ's side
> Wash away my stains,
> Passion of Christ, my comfort be,
> O good Jesus listen to me.
> In your wounds, I fain would hide,
> Ne'er to be parted from your side
> Guard me should the foe assail me,
> Call me when my life shall fail me,
> Bid me come to Thee above,
> With Thy saints, to sing Thy love,
> World without end. Amen.

Prayer before the Sorrowful Face of Jesus

> O Jesus,
> Who in Thy bitter Passion didst become
> The most abject of men, a Man of Sorrows,
> I venerate Thy Sacred Face whereon there once did shine
> The beauty and sweetness of the Godhead.
> But now it has become for me
> As though it were the face of a leper.
> Nevertheless, under these disfigured features
> I recognize Thy infinite love
> And I am consumed with the desire to love Thee

And make Thee loved by all men.
The tears that well up abundantly in Thy eyes
Are to me as so many precious pearls
That I love to gather up
In order to purchase the souls of poor sinners
By means of their infinite value.
O Jesus,
I implore Thee to fix deep within me Thy divine image
And to set me on fire with Thy love
That I may be found worthy
to come to the contemplation
of Thy glorious face in Heaven.
O Blessed Face of my kind Saviour,
By the tender love and piercing sorrow of Your Mother
As she beheld You in Your cruel Passion,
Grant that I may share in this intense sorrow and love,
So as to fulfill the holy will of God
To the utmost of my ability. Amen.

Developing a Practical Routine

The above are not meant to exhaust the possibilities of Christ-centered prayers or ways of praying. There are many others, of course. You have complete freedom in developing your own routine. It may take a little time and some experimentation before you are completely satisfied. And even then, whatever you settle on, you are not bound to permanently; from time to time, you can make whatever changes you wish.

The all-important point is that you must have a routine. Each day you should know precisely what you are expecting—indeed, demanding—of yourself. And you should be intensely faithful in following it—not just to be faithful to a set of prayers or steps, but because these have become a sign of your faithfulness to Christ and a sure way to grow in love for him.

Whatever routine you settle on should be suitable for you. It makes no sense to wind up with one that in many ways may be excellent but provides little satisfaction or simply doesn't work for you. You should not commit yourself to a routine which is too hard, and then try to excuse yourself for not following through with part of it on a particular day by claiming that it was too difficult to begin with; then again, it needs to put sufficient demands on you so that your love for Jesus will in fact grow.

The ideal Christ-centered way for Catholics to pray is by participating at daily Mass and receiving Holy Communion. For many good reasons, however, this will not be feasible for many followers of the Way. But even if it should be, you should have a backup routine for those days when you cannot get to Mass. However, if you cannot or do not wish to incorporate Mass into your routine, you should never look upon whatever else you decide upon as being an inferior way to perform the second step.

If Mass and Holy Communion is not practical, a short visit to the Blessed Sacrament during the day, possibly in conjunction with the Stations of the Cross, may be workable for a few. For most followers of the Matt Talbot Way, however, a practical and effective routine will center around the rosary (five decades). It takes only about fifteen minutes and can be said almost anywhere in conjunction with the ordinary activities of the day. In this sense it is easy: you can never claim that you don't have the time. Most of the other prayers listed here can also be said in the same fashion. Again, the ones you settle on should be memorized.

In evolving a sensible routine, keep in mind that it should

have a certain "weight"; that is, it should require a significant, yet manageable, amount of time and effort as an expression of your dedication to Christ. Your desire to grow in love for him should make you willing to carve out twenty or thirty minutes or so of each day for prayer, even though that dedication is not total in that you are usually able to attend to the other demands of the day at the same time. Of course, if Mass is part of your routine, that alone will take about half an hour.

Here are a few examples of what a practical routine might be:

1. The rosary (five decades) and either or both the Litany of the Sacred Heart and the Angelus.

2. Mass and Holy Communion and the rosary.

3. Mass and Holy Communion and either or both the Litany of the Sacred Heart and the Angelus, together with the rosary.

4. A visit to the Blessed Sacrament, the Stations of the Cross, the Litany of the Sacred Heart, the Angelus, and the rosary.

5. Other Christ-centered prayers of your choice, together with the rosary.

* * *

Prayer for Canonization of Matt Talbot

> Lord, in your servant Matt Talbot you have given us a wonderful example of triumph over addiction, of devotion to duty, and of lifelong reverence for the Most Holy Sacrament. May his life of prayer and penance give us courage to take up our crosses and follow the footsteps of Our Lord and Savior, Jesus Christ.
>
> Father, if it be your will that your beloved servant

should be glorified by your Church, make known by your heavenly favors the power he enjoys in your sight. We ask this through the same Jesus Christ, Our Lord. Amen.

Appendix III

Non-Spiritual Practices

The Matt Talbot Way is a purely spiritual approach in overcoming alcoholism. Because of its spiritual nature, however, the relation of man's physical nature to alcoholism has been purposely ignored. Care has been taken not to sully the spiritual nature of the book by introducing non-spiritual matters into the main body of the text. However, a brief mention should be made of the alcoholic's physical nature, its relationship to alcoholism, and what he can do about it.

His physical makeup may dispose him to alcoholism before he takes his first drink. Once he begins, it may be only a matter of time before he becomes addicted. His addiction may be physical, in that his body craves drink, but more likely it is primarily psychological—he simply thinks he can't get along without it. However, he may also be suffering from depression. This is not the same as the "blue" moods that everyone goes through. If he should be depressed he should get medical help. In any event, the alcoholic's body plays an important role, and if he is to overcome his addiction, it will play a continuing role, even though he follows the purely spiritual steps of the Matt Talbot Way.

Just having his body function without alcohol will make him

feel noticeably better, at least after the initial phase of giving it up. But to increase these good feelings, it is possible that rather simple changes in his daily habits can have a noticeable effect on how easily he adjusts to life without alcohol. These changes involve diet, nutrition, exercise, and rest. By exercise is meant aerobic exercise, such as jogging or vigorous walking, five or six days a week.

He should do more than just learn about these things: he must put them into daily practice. The main obstacle to doing so will probably be his own skepticism or outright disbelief that changes so seemingly insignificant could possibly make much difference. But he is in a position where he has nothing to lose. Rather than take someone else's word that these may help him, or for that matter, the opinion of skeptics who say they will make little or no difference, he can easily find out for himself. All he has to do is put them into practice on a trial basis for a few weeks or so. At the end of that time he can make up his own mind, though possibly well before then he will begin to realize their real worth. Often he will find that indeed they do make a difference. If this should be the case, he should make these changes in habits and practices a permanent part of his life.

He will find that sobriety is no longer something that he must try to hold onto with that white-knuckled desperation that characterizes many reformed alcoholics.

The following books contain practical suggestions that may help the alcoholic to lead a stress-free life without alcohol:

James R. Milam, Ph.D. and Katherine Ketcham. *Under the Influence: A Guide to the Myths and Realities of Alcoholism.* Seattle: Madrona Publishers, 1981.
Janice Keller Phelps, M.D. and Alan E. Nourse, M.D. *The Hidden Addiction and How to Get Free.* Boston: Little, Brown and Company, 1986.

Katherine Ketcham and L. Ann Mueller, M.D. *Eating Right to Live Sober.* Foreword by James R. Milam, Ph.D. Seattle: Madrona Press, 1983.

L. Ann Mueller, M.D. and Katherine Ketcham. *Recovering: How to Get and Stay Sober.* New York: Bantam Books, 1987.

Susan Powter. *Sober... and Staying That Way: The Missing Link in the Cure for Alcoholism.* New York: Simon & Schuster, 1997.

Notes

Chapter I: The Spiritual Dimension
[1] Thomas Wolfe, *Look Homeward, Angel* (New York: Scribner, 1957), 441-42.
[2] H. Reilly, *Easy Does It* (New York: P.J. Kenedy and Sons, 1950), 191.
[3] [Bill Wilson], "Dr. Jung, Dr. Silkworth, and AA," *AA Grapevine*, Vol. 24, No. 8, Jan. 1968, 21.

Chapter II: A Higher Spirituality
[1] Pius XI, "Miserentissimus Redemptor," *The Papal Encyclicals 1903-1939*, ed. Claudia Carlen (McGrath Publishing Co., 1981), 325. Some theologians speculate that the human nature of Jesus did not "know" this sort of thing during his passion. Whether or not he did, however, makes little difference for followers of the Matt Talbot Way; the love which motivates them as they choose to do without drink is always well received by the glorified Christ.

Chapter IV: An Appeal to the Heart
[1] C.S. Lewis, *Letters to Malcolm: Chiefly on Prayer* (New York: Harcourt, Brace, 1963), 89.

Chapter VI: The Matt Talbot Way
[1] An Appeal to the Mother of God is very broadly based on prayers of St. Ildefonsus. See Michael O'Carroll, *Theotokos* (Wilmington, DE: Michael Glazier, Inc., 1982), 177-78. It is a prayer of imitation of Mary, the operative words being "*Teach me* to know and love Him without measure, as you adore Him as Lord and Savior."

Chapter VII: Getting Started
[1] For traditional lives of Christ, good examples are Henri Daniel-Rops, *Jesus and His Times* (Garden City, NY: Doubleday, 1958), and Fulton J. Sheen, *Life of Christ* (New York: McGraw-Hill, 1958). For portraits of Christ based on what are recognized primarily as theological statements of Christian believers as presented in the New Testament, see Donald Senior, *Jesus: A Gospel Portrait* (Dayton, OH: Pflaum Press, 1975), Gerald S. Sloyan, *Jesus in Focus: A Life in its Setting* (Mystic, CT: Twenty-Third Publications, 1983), and Anthony J. Tambasco, *In the Days of Jesus: The Jewish Background and Unique Teaching of Jesus* (New York: Paulist Press, 1983).

No work on the life of Christ can surpass the Gospels themselves. *The Alba House Gospels*, a pocket-size edition of the four Gospels in modern translation, can easily be carried in one's pocket or purse and is highly recommended as is the *St. Paul Catholic Edition of the New Testament*, a colorful fully illustrated edition which includes maps, introductions, the four Gospels, the Acts of the Apostles, the letters of St. Paul, the pastoral letters of Peter, John, Jude and James along with the Letter to the Hebrews and Revelation. The following spiritual aids published by Alba House are also highly recommended: O *Blessed Night* by Francis Kelly Nemeck, OMI and Teresa Coombs, Hermit deals with recovery from addiction, codependency and attachments. *The Normal Alcoholic* by Dr. William F. Kraft offers some help for the "functional" alcoholic.

Chapter XI: The Early Years

[1] Mary Purcell, *Remembering Matt Talbot* (Dublin: Veritas Publications, 1990), 24.
[2] *Ibid.*

Chapter XIII: The Inner Man

[1] Morgan Costelloe, *The Mystery of Matt Talbot* (Dublin: Irish Messenger Publications, 1981), 3.
[2] The value of Matt Talbot's weekly wages, as well as his gifts, is shown in American dollars, although he was paid, of course, in pounds sterling (one pound = $5.00). Before 1915 his weekly pay was about one pound; after 1915, about three pounds.
[3] St. Louis de Montfort, *True Devotion to the Blessed Virgin Mary*, trans. F.W. Faber (Bay Shore, NY: Montfort Publications, 1949), 175-79.

Chapter XIV: Spiritual Motivation

[1] F.J. Sheed, "Matt Talbot," *The Irish Way*, ed. F.J. Sheed (New York: Sheed & Ward, 1934), 327.
[2] Mary Purcell, *Matt Talbot and His Times* (Chicago: Franciscan Herald Press, 1977), 95.
[3] Eddie Doherty, *Matt Talbot* (Milwaukee, WI: Bruce Publishing Company, 1953), 53-54.
[4] G.K. Chesterton, "He Is the Boy," *The Mary Book*, ed. F.J. Sheed (New York: Sheed & Ward, 1951), 264-66.

Chapter XV: Matt's Heroes

[1] Joseph A. Glynn, *Life of Matt Talbot*, 4th ed. (Dublin: Catholic Truth Society of Ireland, 1942), 56.
[2] André Frossard, *"Be Not Afraid"—Pope John Paul II Speaks Out* (New York: St. Martin's Press, 1984), 125.
[3] St. Thérèse of Lisieux, *Autobiography—The Story of a Soul*, trans. R. Knox (New York: P.J. Kenedy & Sons, 1957), 237.
[4] *Ibid.*, 229.
[5] Letter of Thérèse to her sister Céline, August 2, 1893, *Collected Letters of Saint Thérèse of Lisieux*, ed. Abbe Combes, trans. F.J. Sheed (New York: Sheed & Ward, 1949), 197.

Chapter XVI: Matt Talbot Today

[1] St. Thérèse, *Autobiography*, 311.

Chapter XVII. Getting Off Cigarettes

[1] American Cancer Society, 1-800-ACS-2345; American Lung Association, 1-800-LUNG-USA; American Heart Association, 1-800-242-8721.

Chapter XVIII. Controlling Your Weight

[1] François Jamart, *Complete Spiritual Doctrine of St. Thérèse of Lisieux*, Trans. Walter van de Putte (New York: Alba House, 1961), p. 139.

ST PAULS

This book was produced by ST PAULS/Alba House, the Society of St. Paul, an international religious congregation of priests and brothers dedicated to serving the Church through the communications media.

For information regarding this and associated ministries of the Pauline Family of Congregations, write to the Vocation Director, Society of St. Paul, 2187 Victory Blvd., Staten Island, New York 10314-6603. Phone (718) 982-5709; or E-mail: vocation@stpauls.us or check our internet site, www.vocationoffice.org